THE
Timeless
Gospel

THE
Timeless Gospel

HAROLD COOKE PHILLIPS

ABINGDON PRESS
New York • Nashville

THE TIMELESS GOSPEL

Copyright © MCMLVI by Pierce & Washabaugh

Library of Congress Catalogue Card Number: 56-7765

SET UP, PRINTED, AND BOUND BY THE
PARTHENON PRESS, AT NASHVILLE,
TENNESSEE, UNITED STATES OF AMERICA

WITH GRATITUDE AND AFFECTION
TO MY ELDEST BROTHER

George W. Phillips

WHOSE LIFE AND MINISTRY
INSPIRE AND STRENGTHEN ME

Preface

THESE SERMONS ATTEMPT TO DEVELOP A THEME; AND IN this sense they are more like chapters of a book than a miscellaneous collection. Each sermon, however, is complete in itself.

Since both the relevance and truth of the gospel are inseparably connected with the life of Jesus, the first three chapters are centered about him. The first two discuss his uniqueness as seen in his originality and his personality. From his uniqueness results the timelessness of his gospel; this is the theme of the third chapter.

An attempt is then made to relate his message to our contemporary life. We begin with the individual (Chapter Four); not the individual in isolation from his fellows, however—since no such being exists. We are therefore inevitably led to consider some of our social problems and needs in the light of the gospel. One of the criticisms of the gospel is that its goals are unattainable and therefore impractical; an attempt to answer this objection is made in the last chapter.

To George P. Michaelides, a friend of many years and more recently a colleague on the faculty of Oberlin Divinity School, I wish to express my thanks for reading these chapters. His suggestions were always helpful. I also wish to thank my secretary, Miss Gladys Dray, for her painstaking work on this manuscript.

HAROLD C. PHILLIPS

Contents

In a word, if we are not speaking to the needs of the contemporary world, it is a fair guess that we have not really heard the gospel of the early church. On the other hand, however much concern we may have about the contemporary world, that concern is not Christian, except as it stems from the conviction that an event occurred in the first century in the light of which alone the meaning of the contemporary scene can be understood and in the power of which alone the community we seek can be realized. In a word, only an authentic Christianity can be really relevant; only a relevant Christianity can be really authentic.

—JOHN KNOX

I

The Uniqueness of Jesus

"No man ever spoke like this man!"—JOHN 7:46

THE WORD UNIQUE MAY BE DEFINED AS "BEING WITHOUT A like or equal; single in kind or excellence." It seems to me, therefore, that it may be fittingly applied to Jesus. Consider the facts.

Here was a man who worked as a carpenter in a little village in Galilee. He then became an itinerant preacher, and called twelve men to be his disciples. After preaching for three short years—some think even less—he was arrested and falsely charged with certain offenses against the Roman state. He was found guilty and sentenced to death by crucifixion. He died between two thieves, practically friendless, as his disciples had by now deserted him. He left no estate, no writing, or artistic memorial in the field of architecture, painting, or music; not even a house to which people could point and say, "This is where he lived"; for he had "nowhere to lay his head" (Matt. 8:20). By every judgment of common sense this man was destined for oblivion.

Yet what are the facts? The facts are that he who died alone now has millions of followers found in every country on earth. He who wrote nothing, save a few words on the sand, has had more books written about him than any other man who ever lived. "There are more than 2,000 lives of Christ in the British Museum in the English language alone!" [1] Every year the list increases. In the name of the

[1] Kerr, Hugh T., Jr., "Making Old Things New," *Theology Today,* XI (Oct., 1954), 305.

man who died penniless, untold wealth is owned in the form of churches, hospitals, Christian colleges, character-forming agencies, and the like. The man who left no artistic legacy has inspired some of the most beautiful treasures of architecture, painting, music, and literature. In truth, "The very stone which the builders rejected has become the head of the corner." (Matt. 21:42.) As John Knox puts it, "No one else holds or has held the place in the heart of the world which Jesus holds. Other gods have been as devoutly worshiped; no other man has been so devoutly loved." [2]

In view of such facts—incompletely sketched—we are justified, as I think, in calling Jesus a unique person—"without like or equal." Some may not be able to accept the explanation of his uniqueness nor the implications deduced from it, but the fact of it cannot be easily gainsaid. Now we shall consider the uniqueness of Jesus as seen in his originality.

Observe for one thing that his originality has been questioned. No one in Jesus' day seems to have questioned it. "Judea had become a drowsy place, but Jesus by his teaching shook it out of its lethargy and sleep." [3] "No man ever spoke like this man!" said his contemporaries. They called his discourse "a new teaching." If his originality is questioned, there is a reason. It is now generally agreed, strictly speaking, that Jesus said little that could be called new. In his epistle to the Romans, Paul writes, "I am under obligation both to Greeks and to barbarians" (Rom. 1:14). I am sure that Jesus would agree with this statement. Celsus, the second-century critic of Christianity, said that Christ had "raided the wise men of Greece for his wisdom." [4] And if certain of

[2] *The Man Christ Jesus* (Chicago & New York: Willett, Clark & Co., 1941), p. 54.

[3] Jefferson, Charles E., *The Character of Jesus* (New York: Thomas Y. Crowell Co., 1908), p. 95.

[4] Hunter, Archibald M., *Pattern for Life* (Philadelphia: The Westminster Press, 1953), p. 21.

his sayings bear the mark of Greek thought, what shall we say of his indebtedness to Judaism? Here his indebtedness seems well-nigh complete. We are told that there is hardly an ethical insight of Jesus which cannot be paralleled in the Old Testament or other Jewish writings. Let us cite a few examples of this.

One of the most revolutionary of Jesus' insights is his emphasis on the inherent dignity and value of each individual. "For what does it profit a man, to gain the whole world and forfeit his life?" (Mark 8:36.) Yet before Jesus came, one of the rabbis said: "For this reason a single man only (Adam) was created: to teach that if one destroys a single person, the Scripture imputes it to him as if he had destroyed the whole world, and if he saves the life of a single person, as though he had saved the whole world." [5]

If there is one thing in the Gospels which we identify in some peculiar way with Jesus, it is the Lord's Prayer. Our New Testament scholars are now telling us, however, that there is hardly anything in the Lord's Prayer which cannot be found in earlier religions. To be sure the selection, arrángement, and form of the prayer belong to Jesus, but we are told that every single petition can be found somewhere in earlier Jewish liturgies. In view of this and other examples that could be cited, some people find it easy to conclude that Jesus actually brought nothing new but merely repeated in somewhat different form what had already been said, and that, whatever we may say of him, he was not original. His teaching was little more than a "patchwork of quotations."

This statement will not bear examination. It certainly would not be true to say that Jesus brought no new *religious* insights—for he did. Let me remind you of three of them. One was his concept of the kingdom of God. His contempo-

[5] M. Sanhedrin, IV, 5 as quoted in Harry Emerson Fosdick's *Man from Nazareth.*

raries thought of the kingdom as something that was to come; it was all in the future. In Jesus' thought, however, it was not only future but in some sense a present reality; it had come. "The kingdom of God is in the midst of you." (Luke 17:21.) This means that a Christian is a citizen of two worlds—the imperfect world in which he lives, and the world seen in the light of the kingdom with the absolute requirements which Christ revealed.

Another new insight was his concept of God as one who aggressively goes out to seek *the lost*. Some men drifting in a rubber boat on the vast Pacific said the greatest source of strength and hope that came to them during those torturous days was the assurance that they were being sought. Such is Jesus' picture of God—one who seeks the lost. And it was new! Montefiore, the Jewish scholar, says: "The Rabbis . . . welcomed the sinner in his repentance. But to *seek out* the sinner, and, instead of avoiding the bad companion, to choose him as your friend in order to work his moral redemption, this was, I fancy, something new in the religious history of Israel." [6]

There are reputable thinkers who would say that Christ has brought us a new concept of man. Granted, as we have said, that the value of the individual had been recognized; yet Jesus by his life, his teaching about God's seeking love, and supremely by his own death on the cross for us while we were yet sinners, has so enhanced that value as to give us a new concept of man's inherent worth and deathless significance. These then are certain insights of Jesus which may be considered new.

But now observe further that originality cannot be equated with newness. We need not base our claim to Jesus' originality simply on any insights that were peculiarly his. An original thinker is not necessarily one who says what no one

[6] Montefiore, Moses Haim, *The Religious Teachings of Jesus*, p. 57.

else has ever said, but he who sees something new in the old and familiar. He takes truths or ideas which like old coins may be badly shopworn, and, so to speak, remints them so that not only does the old image or superscription appear in bolder relief, but may actually be changed into something new and different. This is constantly happening in every field of human endeavor.

E. F. Scott reminds us that though we speak of the new astronomy or the new physics, the modern astronomer is dealing with the same old stars, and the physicist with laws long familiar to Galileo and Newton. Liberty is an old concept. We of the Western world think back to the days when the Magna Charta was wrung from the hands of King John. Yet this old idea has a new meaning today as we discuss our civil rights.

What is true in the field of science or politics is just as true in the field of literature. No one, I suppose, would question the originality of Shakespeare, and yet we are told that there is little or nothing that is new in his plays. In every one of his plays the great playwright borrowed from the past. Literary critics now know that he took his plots and characters from many sources: Plutarch, Holinshed, and others. Yet those old plots when passed "through the alembic of his mind and, transformed by his genius," became original in the truest sense. As John Lowes writes in his *Convention and Revolt in Poetry:* "In the firsthand comparison of what Shakespeare found and took with the astounding thing he made of it, lies the touchstone of all originality whatsoever." It was Emerson who said, in an overstatement no doubt, that all literature since Plato was a quotation. "I have milked 300 cows," said Oliver Wendell Holmes, Sr., "but I make my own butter."

Now what is true in the areas we have mentioned is especially true of religion. For there is no subject upon which men have brooded so long or deeply. If Jesus had come with a new religious phraseology, he would probably have been little more than a sensational innovator. Jesus recognized his indebtedness to the past when he said that he came not to destroy but to fulfill. "The glory of Christianity," says Jowett, "is not to be as unlike other religions as possible, but to be their perfection and judgment." [7]

With this clarification of originality let us now mention, of necessity, in barest outline, some of Jesus' emphases in which his original contribution to man's religious life may be explored. They have long since been familiar. Yet, familiar though they be, they cannot be overemphasized.

For one thing Jesus viewed his religious tradition with a critical, discriminating mind. He had "an unerring sense of what was important." He differentiated sharply between what was essential and what was of secondary or no importance; between, as he put it, "the weightier matters" and the "mint, anise and cummin." We might say that the religious teaching of his day was comparable to a field in which choice plants of eternal truth were mixed with growths which, if not noxious, were at least scrubby and unfruitful. To his contemporaries, by and large, these were regarded as being of equal worth and so became for the religious, "heavy burdens, hard to bear." Jesus walked over this field with a discriminating mind. Loyal to tradition and yet not enslaved by it, he pointed to the growths of real value and promise and disregarded others. "Every plant which my heavenly Father has not planted will be rooted up." (Matt. 15:13.) As Wellhausen puts it: "The originality of Jesus consists in this that he had the feeling for what was true and eternal amid a chaotic mass of rubbish, and that he enunciated it with the greatest em-

[7] Quoted in Hugh Ross Mackintosh, *The Originality of the Christian Message* (New York: Charles Scribner's Sons, 1920), p. 4. Used by permission of the publisher.

phasis." [8] "But there is a new thing in the Gospels," says the Jewish scholar Klausner. This he finds in the selective capacity of Jesus, his ability to gather together in condensed and concentrated form the important ethical concepts from sources "where they are interspersed among more commonplace discussions and worthless matter." [9] He who has such discernment, the courage to put first things first, breaks new ground —pioneers.

Suppose we had that courage today, the courage to view the religious tradition of our respective churches with the same discrimination! Suppose we had his concern for the "weightier matters" and his lack of concern for the "mint, anise and cummin"! If we had, the unity for which we pray would be more nearly within our reach—if indeed not long since in our possession.

Again. To his capacity for separating the wheat from the chaff, the timeless from the transient, must be added his shifting of man's religious center from the outward act to the inner motive. By and large the religious life of his day had become externalized. Men did their alms and even made their prayers to be seen by men. For many, religion had become a sort of mask. Against this attempt to make of religion an outward form, Jesus made a twofold attack—one positive, the other negative. On the positive side he taught that an act which seemed outwardly good could not be so regarded if prompted by evil motives. To give alms to the poor is surely a commendable act; yet if the motive of such charity be to call attention to one's liberality, the act loses its religious significance. It is prompted by self-love, to be seen of men and praised by them. "Truly, I say to you, they have their reward." (Matt. 6:2.)

[8] Quoted in Archibald M. Hunter, *Pattern for Life* (Philadelphia: Westminster Press, 1954), p. 25.

[9] Quoted in John Knox, *The Man Christ Jesus* (Chicago and New York. Willett, Clark & Co., 1941), p. 35.

He went further than that. If one could not evaluate the religious significance of an act without first knowing the motive behind it, then negatively neither could one who refrained from committing an evil act be considered righteous if he cherished motives which, if acted on, would lead to its committal. One might not commit murder, but if he harbored murderous thoughts he was in reality guilty of it. He might not actually commit adultery, but if he cherished lustful desires it was as though he had. In Jesus' view then, neither the good act that we do nor the evil one we refrain from performing is in and of itself an adequate test of one's religious life. It is the desires of the heart known only to him, who alone seeth in secret, that reveal one's real status. Jesus "internalizes" morality and, in my judgment, justifies the opinion of A. E. Taylor, who says that Christianity stands above all other religions in its inwardness.

This idea may seem rather ordinary to us, so long have we been familiar with it. But its implications for Jesus' day were revolutionary in the extreme, as they are for us today. One who has the insight and the courage to live out this principle of inwardness breaks new ground—pioneers.

So through his discriminating approach and his emphasis on inwardness, Jesus pioneered.

There is a third aspect of the uniqueness of Jesus. We refer to his universalism. This may be seen in his thought of God. When his contemporaries prayed, "Our Father," the words were qualified by racial, social, and religious considerations. In Jesus' thinking, "our" encompassed all mankind. Consider his story of the prodigal son. It begins, "A certain man had two sons" (Luke 15:11 K.J.V.). Who was this man? To what race, nation, or class did he belong? We do not know. He was any man. And no wonder! For this man in the parable is used as a symbol of God, and since Jesus knew God to be the Father of all men, this "certain man" had to remain anonymous. He is more shrouded in anonymity than the unknown

20

soldier in Arlington Cemetery—we know that the soldier was an American.

What was true of his thought of God was equally true of his thought of man. Inevitably so! For the fatherhood of God without its corollary, the brotherhood of man, is an empty phrase. He was once asked: "Who is my neighbor?" His answer was the equally familiar story of the Good Samaritan. Once more we meet the anonymous man. "A certain man went down from Jerusalem to Jericho, and fell among thieves." (Luke 10:30 K.J.V.) Who was this "certain man"? We do not know. It has been pointed out that in telling this story, Jesus let us know the moral or religious state of every character in it save one. The robbers were bad, the priest and Levite were Jews, the Samaritan was a heretic, but the victim on the road—we do not know whether he was a Jew, a Gentile, or a Samaritan; whether he was good or bad, grateful or churlish. All we know is that he was a man in need. So any man anywhere who needs help becomes my neighbor because he is potentially my brother in God. "Your mother and your brothers are standing outside, desiring to see you." And Jesus, looking about him, said, "My mother and my brothers are those who hear the word of God and do it." (Luke 8:20, 21.) He visualized a frontierless kingdom to which "many will come from east and west and sit at table with Abraham, Isaac, and Jacob in the kingdom of heaven" (Matt. 8:11).

That a man who never traveled more than fifty to a hundred miles from the place where he was born, should have been so completely free from any taint of provincialism or the particularisms of race, class, or nation, is an amazing fact—a unique fact. One who lives in the light of that truth breaks new ground—pioneers.

We have been trying to point out some of the emphases or insights of Jesus which substantiate the claim to his originality. And yet perhaps the most important thing cannot be put in words. The deepest truths can never be—we feel them.

21

All sympathetic readers of the Gospels sense in them a freshness, a newness. To move from the Old to the New Testament is like coming down in a train from the lofty, beautiful but austere snow-covered heights of the Sierras into the warmer climate, more intimate, luxuriant beauty of the Sacramento Valley. The coming of Jesus, like that of spring, clothed the old familiar landscape with a new beauty. The originality of Jesus is comparable to that of a great artist who, although using the familiar basic colors, yet through his creative artistry fashions something more beautiful than hitherto produced. One is reminded of the story of an antiquarian. He was pointing out to a sculptor friend that there was nothing original about Greek sculpture, since its characteristic features had appeared in the art of the Egyptians, Assyrians, and Hittites. He therefore concluded that the Greeks had, in fact, invented nothing. "Nothing," replied the other, "except the beautiful."

It would not be fair to say that nowhere in the Old Testament does one catch glimpses of this beauty. One does! Take universality, for example. It was surely foreshadowed in the Old Testament! One sees it in the book of Jonah and others of the prophets. Isaiah spoke of God as one to whom every knee would bow. (Isa. 45:23.) So, too, the other insights we have discussed. But this must be said: what is occasional in the Old Testament is continuous in the New; what in the Old Testament seems like candlelight, in the New Testament is sunlight; what in the Old Testament is a voice crying in the wilderness, in the New Testament becomes a chorus rising to a grand crescendo. Moreover—and how important this is— what in the Old Testament is a word, in the New is a Word made flesh, Truth incarnate in a life. We confront in the New Testament not just a true idea, but a man in whom truth lives. "The words that I have spoken to you are spirit and life" (John 6:63) : "The life was the light of men" (John 1:4) . This is one facet of the uniqueness of Jesus.

II

What Sort of Man Is This?

"Thou art the Christ, the Son of the living God."
—MATT. 16:16 K.J.V.

WE HAVE SAID THAT THERE WERE TWO ANGLES FROM which we would consider the uniqueness of Jesus. We have spoken of one of them, his originality. We now turn to the other, his personality. "The only new thing that ever enters into this world is a human personality." [1] To the question, "What new thing did Jesus give?" Irenaeus answered, "He brought all that was new, in bringing Himself." [2]

It would be more than presumptuous to try to discuss the personality of Jesus within the limits of a sermon. Of course, we are making no such attempt. Rather, let us mention four words, key words, which, as I see them, open doors through which the uniqueness of his personality may be explored. "What sort of man is this?" asked the disciples. These key words suggest, in part at least, where we may seek the answer.

The first word is *centrality.* Jesus stands at the center of the New Testament. Christianity could well-nigh be defined in three words: *Christianity is Christ.* The gospel is bound not in a book, but in a life. It may be said that every great religion revolves about the personality of its founder. In Christianity, however, this is true to a degree and in a sense not found else-

[1] E. F. Scott, *The Lord's Prayer* (New York: Charles Scribner's Sons, 1951, p. 72.
[2] Quoted in James S. Stewart, *A Man in Christ* (New York: Harper & Bros.) , p. 76.

23

where. Solomon B. Freehof, a distinguished Jewish preacher writes: "No Moslem ever sings, 'Mohammed, lover of my soul,' nor does any Jew say of Moses, the Teacher, 'I need thee every hour,' . . . He brought God near to men through his presence. He made the Divine personal for myriads of worshipers." [3] Or as Phillips Brooks put it, "To me, the gospel is just one great Figure standing with outstretched arms." [4]

Moreover, the centrality of Jesus' personality was his own idea. He deliberately put himself at the center of his message. This, too, is unique. Socrates, perhaps the rarest soul of antiquity, said, "If you will take my advice, you will think little of Socrates, and a great deal more of truth." Jesus on the contrary said, "I am . . . the truth"; "Come unto me"; "Follow me"; "Learn of Me."

The claims he makes for himself, even to identifying himself with God, are astonishing. Even more astonishing is the fact that those who know him, find in such claims not the slightest trace of egotism or presumption. If the sun should say, "I am the light of the solar system," no star within that system would, so to speak, raise its eyebrows in resentment or astonishment. No more do Christians when the Christ of the Fourth Gospel says, "I am the light of the world." For, in truth, we are convinced that that is precisely what he is.

Perhaps not the least reason for our conviction is that "though he was in the form of God (he) did not count equality with God a thing to be grasped, but emptied himself, taking the form of a servant." (Phil. 2:6-7.) In John's Gospel he is reported to have said, "The Father is greater than I." (John 14:28.) "The Father who dwells in me does his work" (John 14:10). In Mark he says, "Why do you call me good? No one is good but God alone" (Mark 10:18). Such statements indicate that his life was one of complete subordination

[3] *Stormers of Heaven* (New York: Harper & Bros., 1931), pp. 210, 211.

[4] Quoted in Charles Clayton Morrison, *The Unfinished Reformation* (New York: Harper & Bros., 1953), p. 195.

and obedience to the will of his Father. This very selflessness is not the least of the qualities for which men have exalted him and given him "the name which is above every name." (Phil. 2:9.)

It is not surprising that the New Testament should be centered in a life rather than a book; for its supreme truth without which, like a wheel without the hub, all of its teaching would be at loose ends, is the incarnation of God in Christ. "God was in Christ." (II Cor. 5:19). "The Word became flesh" (John 1:14). Only by making Christ central, can the major truth of the gospel be given its rightful place of primacy. If that place of centrality were usurped, we should be giving to some lesser truth a position which rightly belongs to the greatest one.

The second word we suggest as a possible key to the uniqueness of Jesus' personality is *reality*. Whatever we may conceive reality to be, one thing is certain—Jesus was in touch with it, embodied it.

This is seen in his dealings with people. With unerring insight he grasped the realities of human life. "He himself knew what was in man" (John 2:25). He had an uncanny way of sizing up people, sensing their inmost thoughts, their hidden motives, and their needs. The modern psychiatrist or psychoanalyst uses a vocabulary that would have been strange to his ears. But one wonders if either has surpassed, nay, caught up with Jesus in analyzing the cause of personality disorders and their possible cure. Jesus saw the treachery of Judas, the fickleness of Peter, the dishonesty of Zacchaeus, the selfishness of the Rich Young Ruler, the cold respectability of Nicodemus, the moral lapses of the Samaritan woman, more clearly than they themselves did. Knowing the sin in man, he was even more convinced of the inherent possibilities of the most unpromising recipient of God's redeeming love and grace.

But if Jesus knew what was in man, the individual, he was

25

just as unerring in appraising the evils that plague society. Time has proved and is constantly verifying the truth of his social insights. Here, too, he was dealing with realities. His teachings concerning the dignity and worth of man as a child of God, the possession and use of money, the futility of force, the obligation to use power for service rather than overlord-ship, his view of brotherhood, no longer a luxury, but as time is proving a necessity for survival—these and similar insights are no less true today than when he voiced them; they are more true. Time is showing that we betray them at our peril, if not our destruction. Once when Jesus was teaching in the temple and claiming for his new teaching the authority of truth, his hearers asked, "How is it that this man has learning, when he has never studied?" He replied, "My teaching is not mine, but his who sent me." And he added, "If any man's will is to do his will, he shall know whether the teaching is from God or whether I am speaking on my own authority" (John 7:15-17).

This brings us to the heart of the matter. Jesus has done more to make us aware of the reality of God than anyone who ever lived. The secret of this lies not just in what he said about God; it lies rather in his own God-consciousness. God was more real to Jesus than all else—so real that in seeing and hearing him, his disciples came to believe that they were in touch with God himself. Browning once likened "the revela-tion of God in the universe to an isosceles triangle, the two equal sides of which, *strength* and *intelligence,* are clear enough; but the base of which, *goodness,* is not in sight." That base the poet found in Jesus:

> I say, the acknowledgment of God in Christ
> Accepted by thy reason, solves for thee
> All questions in the earth and out of it.[5]

[5] Quoted in Richard Roberts, *That One Face* (New York: Association Press, 1919), p. 96.

In speaking of his God-consciousness, Hugh Ross Mackintosh says:

It seized men with fresh elemental power and passed like fire from heart to heart. For the first time the warm unforgettable realities of a man's life are the index of the Unseen. . . . Hence to realise the new thought of God, what is chiefly required is not a grammar or lexicon—not even a Biblical Theology; it is to stand before Jesus' life, as before a great picture, and let its meaning take possession of us. A distinctive revelation of the Father is given by His life.[6]

It was Jesus' contact with God that gave him the authority he possessed. When he spoke, men caught an accent of assurance and certainty which was unique. "There was never a quiver in his voice." He was in no sense an authoritarian, but spoke with authority: "Verily, verily, I say unto thee." His was the authority of embodied truth.

We have spoken of the centrality of Jesus' personality and of its reality. Let us now consider a third key word—*vitality*. Not only was he a real person, but a vital person. It was H. G. Wells who said, "The historian's test of an individual's greatness is 'What did he leave to grow? Did he start men to thinking along fresh lines with a vigor that persisted after him?' By this test Jesus stands first." We might say that if Moses was the lawgiver, Christ is the life-giver. The Christ of the Fourth Gospel says, "I came that they may have life, and have it abundantly." (John 10:10.)

He must have possessed physical vitality. Few now doubt his miracles of healing. He who imparted or restored life must have himself possessed it.

There was vitality in the way he taught. He did not leave a set of rules that men might outgrow, but of principles to be explored. There was nothing stereotyped, cut and dried, about

[6] Hugh Ross Mackintosh, *The Originality of the Christian Message* (New York: Charles Scribner's Sons, 1920), p. 53. Used by permission.

his presentation of truth. Moreover, he never imposed his ideas on others, but tried to stimulate their own thinking. He asked questions, the answers to which tested his hearers' creative powers. When he was questioned, he seldom gave a direct answer. His answer was another question, as though he wanted his hearers to think for themselves. He did not say, "Copy me," but, "Follow me." His concept of truth was not static but dynamic, not lifeless but resilient. As we read his parables, profound in their simplicity, we see how he relates eternal truth to current issues: the expectancy of fishermen who cast their nets into the sea, the concern of the shepherd who seeks a lost sheep, the greed of the vinedressers who stopped at nothing—not even murder—and the tragedy of the rich man whose soul grew smaller as his barns grew bigger. These and similar teachings show that at the heart of his message was always some vital, living issue. Indeed, it was the vitality of his message that aroused hostility against him. The leaven worked in the lump—"He stirs up the people" (Luke 23:5) — the old wineskins could not contain the new wine.

Furthermore he never gave his followers the feeling that they had heard the last word or reached the end of the line. He told them that there were many things he still wanted to say to them, but that they were not ready. He would send the Spirit of truth, who would lead them into all truth and show them things to come.

Such in brief are some of the marks of the vitality of Jesus' earthly ministry.

That ministry lasted but three short years, and then Jesus was crucified. It occurred to no one who saw him die—least of all to the disciples, who could not stomach the scene and so had run away—but that he was witnessing the last act of a tragic drama, the falling of the final curtain. Fall the curtain did, but, as history shows, only to rise again on a drama of vaster proportions. His enemies actually thought they could stop by killing him. In this they were mistaken! "Here lies" are words inscribed on the tombs of the world's greatest men. "He is not here" are the words on Jesus' grave. Death did not destroy the vitality of his life. On the contrary, it immeasurably increased it. Jesus may have had this in mind when he said, "Unless a grain of wheat falls into the earth and dies, it remains alone; but if it dies, it bears much fruit" (John 12:24). As one of our New Testament scholars writes:

The Gospel is thoroughly definite; but it is quick with life, and like all living things it exists not as a finished immobile entity, but as a vital impulse never to be spent. To one age it has given a new sense of God, to another, a fresh idea of personal devotion, to a third a social conscience. . . . Perhaps the greatest thing in Christianity is that you never know what it will do next. At any moment it may break out at a new place—seizing on some imperfectly evangelised aspect of life and moulding it to a higher likeness.[7]

You have no doubt recognized behind each of these untechnical words we have used so far in describing the personality of Jesus, an enduring theological truth. For example, behind the word *centrality* is the person of Christ. The apostles did not go out preaching the Golden Rule, the Sermon on the Mount, or the ethical teachings of Jesus. "We preach Christ crucified," (I Cor. 1:23.) they said. That was central in their message.

Similarly, behind the word *reality* lies the truth of revelation. We believe that in Christ, God has revealed the truth about man and his world; yea, more—the truth of his own nature. Christ is the revelation of reality.

In like manner the word *vitality* expresses in everyday language the power of his resurrection. "What did he leave to grow?" asks Mr. Wells. He left the church to grow. The church, the body of Christ, the new covenant, was founded on

[7] *Ibid.,* pp. 25-26. Used by permission.

29

his life and death, his body and blood. But it is no monument to a departed hero. It bears witness to the continuing presence and power of the risen Christ in the lives of men and women.

Now when we put these three words and the truths they represent together, they suggest a fourth word as a key to Jesus' personality. It is the word *redemptive*. This word embodies all the others. From the first century until now, men have looked to him as their redeemer from sin, suffering, and death itself. In the redemptive power of his personality the uniqueness of Jesus reveals its most Godlike quality. Suffice it now that we make one or two observations on this great theme which, implied when not explicitly stated, underlies all that is said in this book.

In *Cry, the Beloved Country* Alan Paton says, "The tragedy is not that things are broken. The tragedy is that they are not mended again." Jesus possessed the unique power of healing and redeeming men. This was central in his teaching. He described his mission in these words: "The Son of man came to seek and to save the lost" (Luke 19:10). No parable comes closer to the heart of his message than that of the lost sheep. He said he was sent to the lost sheep of the house of Israel. He assured men that they could be born again. "Behold, I make all things new." (Rev. 21:5.)

What he preached, he practiced. When the imprisoned John sent messengers to question his credentials, he replied: "Go and tell John what you have seen and heard: the blind receive their sight, the lame walk, lepers are cleansed, and the deaf hear, the dead are raised up, the poor have good news preached to them." (Luke 7:22.) The lives he touched were changed. Fishermen became fishers of men. Weak, unstable men like Peter became rock-like in character. Grafters like Zacchaeus were made honest; and men like Thomas, who began by doubting him, ended up by being willing to die for him.

When he left the world, his redemptive work did not stop.

Then it really began. The experience of Paul reveals its time-less power. He was a scholar, familiar with the treasures of rabbinical literature. Yet he confessed that in Christ—whom he probably had never seen in the flesh—he found that for which he had previously sought in vain. He found new life. "If any one is in Christ, he is a new creation; the old has passed away, behold, the new has come." (II Cor. 5:17.) Perhaps Paul was thinking of the transformation wrought in him when he spoke of "the mystery of Christ" (Col. 4:3). We shall not attempt to solve the mystery. We shall only say that Christ made God so real and near that after he left the world, the apostles believed that to possess his spirit was to experience the redemptive power of God in human life, and so do we. "The Lord is the Spirit." (II Cor. 3:17.)

The secret of his redemptive power lies in his cross. Lamennais said, "All that Christ asked of the world where-with to save it, was a cross whereon to die." But there was something unique about his cross! If the cross, the most dreaded and degrading symbol of the pagan world, has be-come our most revered symbol, it is because we believe that what transpired there was not simply an affair between men. "Were you there when they crucified my Lord?" Well, God was there! "God was in Christ reconciling the world to him-self." (II Cor. 5:19.) It is because we believe that in the suf-fering of Christ we see God's concern for us, and in the love of Christ a revelation of God's unwearied love, that the cross is for us the matchless symbol of God's redemptive power and love.

That redemptive work begun in the first century has been going on ever since. It will not stop until God has fulfilled "the eternal purpose which he has realized in Christ Jesus our Lord" (Eph. 3:11). Walter Horton puts it vividly:

A stone thrown into a pond creates waves which are practically imperceptible before they reach the shore. A shout thrown into the air re-echoes for a few moments, then dies away forever. But the life of Jesus, sacrificially thrown into the lives of his disciples, kindled there a new life that has never died away, and never will." [8]

And so we think of Jesus as a unique person. Unique in what he said. Unique in what he was. Unique in that he was what he said. In his cross the teacher and his teaching become one and inseparable. "What sort of man is this?" Christians adown the ages have found but one adequate answer: "Thou art the Christ, the Son of the living God."

[8] *Our Eternal Contemporary* (New York: Harper & Bros., 1942), p. 125.

III

The Inescapable Question

"Then what shall I do with Jesus who is called Christ?"
—MATT. 27:22

IT IS NATURAL THAT WE SHOULD ASSOCIATE THE INESCAPABLE
with death. Job's question, "If a man die, shall he live again"
(Job 14:14) is an inescapable question, for die we surely shall.
Death is inescapable. Let me suggest, however, that life is just
as inescapable as death. If it is true that we must die, it is just
as true that we must live. Indeed, life is more inescapable
than death since it precedes death. If we did not live, we
could not die.

Now whenever we think of life, we think of Christ. It is
significant that the two major days on the church's calendar
—Christmas and Easter—suggest life. At Christmas we sing,
"Joy to the world! the Lord is come." We commemorate the
birth of Jesus. At Easter we sing, "Christ the Lord is risen today, Alleluia!" We commemorate his second birthday—his
triumph over death. Christ then is a symbol of life, the life
that is and the one we believe is to come. Peter voiced the
faith of the church when he wrote, "It was not possible
for him to be held by it (death)" (Acts 2:24). And
Paul, too, when he said that Christ had "brought life
and immortality to light" (II Tim. 1:10). Since Christ
is our symbol of life, Pilate's question has timeless significance: "Then what shall I do with Jesus who is called Christ?"
(Matt. 27:17). Our answer affects life both here and here-
after.

Observe in the first place that for Pilate at least this was an inescapable question. He had Jesus on his hands and he had to do something with him. If ever a man tried to wiggle out of a decision, Pilate did. You will remember how hard he tried. Pilate told those determined that Jesus should die that Jesus was innocent. He found no fault in him. That did not work. He sent him to Herod, hoping that he might pass sentence. But that failed. He gave the crowd a choice between Barabbas, a notorious robber, and Christ. They chose Barabbas. So all his efforts failed. He then took water and washed his hands. But washing his hands did not remove his responsibility for making a decision about his prisoner. There he stood. Pilate still had to answer the question.

How he eventually answered his question we know. He must have argued, "If I cannot get rid of him politely, diplomatically, I shall do it brutally and finally, once and for all." And he did. He sentenced him to death!

Now this method of getting rid of those that trouble us has proved to be a very speedy and effective one. How well the Communists know that! The methods they employ were the very ones used on Jesus. Arrest, trumped-up charges, a mock trial, death. But there the similarity ends. We cannot add, as do the Communists: "And so we got rid of him." For killing Jesus did not get rid of him.

How do we know it did not get rid of him? Paul's experience on the Damascus road is part of the answer. This experience with the living Christ changed his life and thus the life of his world. Carey in India, Judson in Burma, Grenfell in Labrador, Schweitzer in Africa: these modern apostles are all proof of the continuing presence and power of the living Christ. So is our presence here. We do not gather in our churches Sunday after Sunday to conduct memorial services, but to proclaim our faith in One who "liveth, and was dead: and (is) alive for evermore." (Rev. 1:18 K.J.V.) Since this is so, the question Pilate faced and had to answer becomes our question, too: "Then what shall I do with Jesus?" Well, what are *we* doing with him? We do not like to face that question any more than Pilate did. Like Pilate we are trying to get rid of him so we shall not have to answer it. Let us see how many of us moderns are trying to get rid of Jesus.

Many years ago Harry Emerson Fosdick preached a sermon entitled "The Peril of Worshiping Jesus." He showed, as only he could, how we are tempted to make adoration of Jesus a substitute for facing the challenge of the gospel. We get rid of him by calling him, "Lord, Lord," yet ignoring the things that he says. Or, we put him safely away in orthodox creeds which we repeat, failing the while to carry out their implications in our daily lives. We honor him with our lips while our lives are far from him. Unquestionably, this way of getting rid of Jesus—paying him lip service—is still used. Let us consider some other ways.

Some of us try to get rid of Jesus by saying he is outdated. The argument goes something like this: Here was a man who lived nineteen hundred years ago. He lived in a tiny country which geographically and politically was of small consequence. How unsophisticated he was! How almost naïve in the simplicity of his life! He was entirely devoid of all the technical and scientific knowledge which has changed the face of the earth—the face of it, mark you, not the heart of it. He never used any of the amazing gadgets with which we are so enamored. He knew nothing of horsepower—just man power. His fastest means of transportation was a rowboat. He never traveled more than fifty to a hundred miles from the place where he was born. In the light of all this he is about as behind the times as anyone could be. Jesus may have been all right for first-century Palestine, but he is surely a misfit in twentieth-century America. And so when the question is asked, "Then what shall I do with Jesus?" those who share this view reply: "Why, nothing. He belongs to another age. He is outdated."

Such victims of modernity have we become, that one can understand this attitude. Has there ever been an age when things become so quickly outdated as they do in our age? Nothing remains new for long; it is soon replaced by something newer. Indeed, our industrial economy feeds on this ever-growing desire of the public for the newest and latest. "Get the latest model else you won't be in style, and what could be worse than to be considered out-of-date?" Some of us unfortunately carry this over even into the realm of ideas, naïvely assuming that the newest must be the truest, that wisdom was born with us.

Now the sobering fact is that all our eagerness for the newest and latest, all the gadgets of modernity, have had but little effect upon our life. They are like the surf and sud of the shore, that leave untouched the secret depths of the ocean. They have increased our speed, but have not changed our direction; they have given us more facile ways of expressing ourselves, but have not changed at all the self which we express; they have revealed our cleverness, but not added to our wisdom. To think that because the Master lived in a pre-scientific age, he has no word for our age is really not to think at all. Jesus moved in the deep areas of life. He revealed life's unchanging realities. This is why his message, though timeless, is always timely. "I have never come up to thee, modern as I am," wrote George Matheson. Nor have we. "In him was life, and the life was the light of men." (John 1:4.) It still is. It always will be.

Once more. We sometimes try to get rid of Jesus not by saying he is outdated, but rather by saying he is impractical. He just was not tough enough for the realities of this world. He handled people with kid gloves when actually they ought to be handled with brass knuckles. He looked at life—it seems—through rose-colored glasses. He talked too much about birds, flowers, and the beauty of the sunsets. He grew too sentimental about the poor, the sick, the underprivileged, and little children. He was not sufficiently aware of the actualities of life; he was too much concerned with its possibilities. He did not see people as they really were, so obsessed was he with the idea of what they might become. His whole scale of values was wrong. He said the greatest people were not those who strutted or selfishly lorded it over others, but those who assumed the role of a servant, who sought not to be ministered unto but to minister. He said a human life was more valuable than the whole world, and that only those of a childlike spirit could enter the kingdom of heaven. And to top it all off, he said that the greatest power in the world was not brute force; not, as we now think, the power of the hydrogen bomb, but love. He is impractical. When therefore we are asked, "What shall I do with Jesus" we, too, answer, "Nothing. He is a dreamer who cherished beautiful ideals which just will not work in this age of brutal facts."

This argument has some truth. Let us admit that the absolute ethic of Jesus, the ethic of love, just does not fit into a world like this. But that is just the point. Who wants to live in a world like this? It is becoming evident that unless we change our ways, either there will not be much world left to live in or at least not many people left to live in it. Anyone who considers our world today, tied up in knots, paralyzed with fear, poisoned with hate and suspicion, and skating on the brink of possible destruction, and then says that our way of life is practical and Jesus a sentimental dreamer—such a person must be blind. It is *he* who is viewing life through rose-colored glasses.

No, we cannot get rid of Jesus by calling him impractical. Slowly but surely we are coming to see that his gospel is hard-headed common sense, that only the leaven of his gospel can change the lump of life which has gone sour. As the late Willard L. Sperry has written:

The one sin for which there is no forgiveness in this whole realm of Christian concern is that of skepticism as to the ultimate power of the Christian ideal to work its own final victories in our world. . . . To lose faith in the ultimate efficacy of the spirit of Christ, manifest in his moral teaching, and to cease upholding the prophetic vision of a Christian order . . . is to sin the sin against the Holy Spirit for which there is not and, in the very nature of the case, cannot be any forgiveness.[1]

There is yet another way in which we try to get rid of Jesus. We just ignore him. We go about our business from day to day as if Jesus had never lived, as though he had never died and conquered death. This is a quite effective method of getting rid of anything. More things perish from neglect than from aggressive assault. Yet I wonder if Halford Luccock is not right when he says, "We can no more escape Jesus by ignoring him than we can escape dying by ignoring death." [2]

The truth of this becomes evident when we consider the influence Christ has had on our culture. Anyone who attempts to write a history of Western civilization and omits the influence of Christ would discard the main key to its meaning. Our hospitals, colleges, our character-forming agencies, our great humanitarian movements—is there one of these that has not been influenced directly or indirectly by the life and teachings of Jesus? Why do such things not exist in countries where he is unknown? Indeed, think even of our voting booths, where we express our choices as free men. Are we aware of the part that the Christian gospel with its emphasis on the dignity and worth of each individual has had in the establishment of democracy? Why are there not similar booths behind Iron Curtains? Emerson was right when he said that the name of Jesus was not written but plowed into history.

[1] Willard L. Sperry, *The Discipline of Liberty* (New Haven: Yale University Press, 1921) , p. 96. Used by permission of the publisher.

[2] *Interpreter's Bible* (Abingdon Press: New York and Nashville, 1951) , VII, 897.

Mark Twain put it stronger. In 1871 he wrote: "All that is great and good in our particular civilization came straight from the hand of Jesus Christ." [3] We can ignore him, but no one who lives in our culture can escape him by ignoring him. We may be isolated from the Christian movement, but we cannot be insulated from it. We can try to blot Christ out of our individual lives, but that does not mean that we do blot him out!

It is evident then that we are no more successful than Pilate in trying to get rid of Jesus. Calling him outdated, impractical, even ignoring him, does not get rid of him. The inescapable question remains: "Then what shall I do with Jesus?"

Let us ask now, Why can't we get rid of Jesus? Why was not the Cross or the tomb in Joseph's garden the end of him? Why has no tyrant to date been able to kill his church or stamp out his religion? How do we explain the fact that our Caesars, Alexanders, Napoleons, Hitlers, Stalins, and all the rest have their day and cease to be, like falling meteors that attract our attention momentarily ere they sink to darkness and oblivion, while this man shines on and on like some morning star, holding out to each succeeding generation the promise of a brighter day? Why is Jesus just as live an issue and a far more widespread one today than in the first-century world? A story Leslie Weatherhead tells gives about as simple and satisfying an answer as possible.

It is about a five-year-old boy who used to listen to the radio, but understood very little of what he heard. He could understand the children's programs, but other programs were beyond him. He observed that his parents listened every day to what they called "the news," but of this he could make nothing. One Sunday morning the little boy went into his mother's bedroom where the radio had been turned low so as not to disturb the baby, and someone was talking. He as-

[3] Quoted in Edward Wagenknecht, *Mark Twain, the Man and his Work* (New Haven: Yale University Press, 1935), p. 206.

sumed it was "the news." But this Sunday morning a word continually cropped up which he had not noticed before. It was the word "God." He ran down to the kitchen where his grandmother was preparing dinner and said, "Granny, you had better turn on the radio. It's the news, but today it's about God."

I do not know of any simpler or more profound answer to our question than that. We cannot get rid of Jesus because he is the news about God. We cannot get rid of Jesus unless we first get rid of God, and that we cannot do. "God was in Christ reconciling the world to himself." (II Cor. 5:19.) To say this is surely not to say that God has never been in other men. The New Testament tells us that "in many and various ways God spoke of old to our fathers" (Heb. 1:1). But what they said was not said with the completeness, was not as convincing, shall we say as winsome, as what Jesus uttered. Was this partly because while the prophets gave us truths, we believe that in Christ we have the truth—the truth about ourselves, about our relationships with our fellows and our relationship to God? We believe, in short, that there is something cosmic about Christ, that as the apostle says, "in him all things hold together." (Col. 1:17.)

And we believe this because without such faith, we cannot account for the unparalleled influence of the life of Christ in history nor for his continuing power in the world today. In a unique sense Christ is God's man. His greatest contribution to humanity is that he has made God real and brought him near. What we do about Jesus, then, we do about God. When he was crucified long ago, it was not just the carpenter from Nazareth men had to reckon with, they had to reckon with God.

This leads us to make a final observation. What a man does about God does not so much affect God as it does the man himself. Whenever we pass judgment on that which transcends us, we are actually passing judgment on ourselves.

When we profane beauty, we are not revealing anything about beauty but about ourselves. When we spurn goodness, we are not defaming the character of goodness, but our character. When we betray truth, it is not truth that is disgraced —we are. Whenever we sit in judgment on that which is better than we are—purer, nobler, more godlike than we are— we sit in judgment on ourselves. In the first century it was thought that Pilate was judging Jesus. Now we know better. We know that in passing judgment on Jesus, he was only revealing to endless generations the kind of man he was. In passing judgment on Christ, he was actually passing judgment on himself.

And so are we!

When, for example, we ignore his teaching concerning purity of life, disciplined self-control, or the sacredness of personality, we sentence ourselves to some far country where the beauty of life turns to ashes at our touch.

To refuse Christ's offer of God's forgiving love and redeeming grace is to carry a load of guilt on our conscience.

To think his faith in a God who loves us, whom we can trust, on whom we can cast our burdens, too naïve, is to expose ourselves to anxiety neuroses.

To live without faith in his resurrection is to live without the "lively hope" that gives meaning to our mortal days.

"Then what shall I do with Jesus?" Accept him. Believe in him. Try to follow him.

Let me make a personal confession. I do not know how you feel about this, but this is how I feel about it. Should our faith in Christ turn out to be misplaced; if he was mistaken when he taught that God, the Ultimate Reality, is love; if he was wrong in his emphasis on the inherent dignity and worth of every human life in the sight of God; if he "missed the boat" when he said that all men were brothers in God, or that forgiveness, good will and service unlocked the door to life; if his vision of a redeemed world, the kingdom of God, the rule of righteousness and love, was a pious dream: if he was wrong in all this, I would rather be wrong with him than be right with those who betrayed him. I would rather be wrong with Jesus than right with Judas.

It is our faith that Jesus was not mistaken. "The light shines in the darkness, and the darkness has not overcome it." (John 1:5.) Nay, rather it has only made it more luminous. There is, I suppose, no greater reason for believing the truth of the gospel than that time is on its side—verifies it. Nothing has happened in nineteen hundred years to discredit the insights of Jesus. On the contrary, each recurring crisis but confirms them. Let me remind you of a story Harry Emerson Fosdick tells in one of his books. It concerns a group of medical research scientists who were discussing one of their number recently deceased.

They spoke of his zeal for truth and his competence as a scientist; they spoke of the opposition and incredulity he had met and of his courage in facing it, until one of the group said this: "He was wrong for so long, and then he turned out to be right." [4]

That will be history's verdict on Jesus: "He turned out to be right." It is history's verdict already for those who see.

---

[4] *A Faith for Tough Times* (New York: Harper & Bros., 1952), p. 57.

IV

On Being One's Self

"When he came to himself he said, . . . I will arise and go to my father." —LUKE 15:17, 18

IT IS SAID OF ONE OF OUR BEST-KNOWN MOVING-PICTURE DI-rectors that his greatest problem with young actors is to keep them from trying to become second-rate Lana Turners or third-rate Clark Gables instead of just being themselves. This problem is not peculiar to Hollywood. Many of us are loath to accept ourselves for what we are. We pretend to be what we are not and so end up by being anomalous personalities, neither the person we really are nor the one we pretend to be. Rabbi Zusya said, "In the coming world they will not ask me: 'Why were you not Moses?' They will ask me: 'Why were you not Zusya?' " [1] This, however, does not get to the heart of the matter. For the deeper question is, "Who or what is Zusya? When is he being himself?"

This question could be easily answered if the self were one. But that is just what it is not. "I should know myself better if there were not so many of me." Every conscientious person is aware of the inner conflict between his lower and his higher self. Paul voiced it when he said, "I see in my members an-other law at war with the law of my mind and making me cap-tive to the law of sin which dwells in my members" (Rom. 7:23). The effort then to be one's self involves more than a refusal to imitate others. What does it require?

[1] Quoted in Herrymon Maurer, *What Can I Know?* (New York: Harper & Bros., 1953), p. 239.

In the first place, to be one's self requires a decision. Each of us has to make up his own mind which self, the good or the evil, is really he. What belongs by right in the garden of our life, flowers or weeds? Who is the trespasser, good or evil? If, as Phillips Brooks suggested, life like a checkerboard has white and black spots, is the board basically white with the black spots an intrusion, or black with the white spots horning in? In whose image are we made, the image of God or the devil?

In our everyday experience we have no difficulty in making this decision. Instinctively we identify the real with the best. For example, we hear a famous singer and are disappointed. "He is not in voice tonight," we say; that is, not himself, not at his best. If the pitcher who usually "mows 'em down" is knocked out of the box, we say, "He just did not have it to-day"—that is, he was not himself, not at his best. If some friend of ours whose spirit is usually buoyant seems depressed or morose we say, "John did not seem himself today." In such and similar instances we instinctively identify the real with the best.

Now can we apply this test not just to how a man functions or even to his physical condition, but to himself, his character? Some years ago an eastern paper carried the picture of a mother who had abandoned her baby—left the child on a doorstep. Not long after the same paper carried the picture of the American mother chosen that year for her motherly virtues. Which of these mothers more truly reveals the real self?

Here is an exploiter or arrogant bigot who regards the Africans as pawns to his economic greed or racial illusions. Here is Albert Schweitzer, whose brotherly love and amazing service lighten up the dark continent. Again the question re-curs—which of these two men reveals human nature?

Jesus, steadfast optimist that he was, would be in no doubt about the answer. He saw more clearly than any the

44

evil in man, but never regarded it as an expression of his true nature. He told a story once of a boy, the Prodigal Son, who went into the far country and wasted his substance in riotous living. He kept going from bad to worse. But said the Master, "When he came to himself he said, '. . . I will arise and go to my father.' " (Luke 15:18.) So our Lord taught that a man enslaved by sin—ideals gone, decency gone, character gone—simply was not being himself. Jesus believed that the real self is the best self, that the deepest thing in man is his kinship with his Father. John Ruskin is voicing the view of the Master when he writes in his *Crown of Wild Olives:*

All of the sin of men I esteem as their disease, not their nature; as a folly which may be prevented, not a necessity which must be accepted. And my wonder, even when things are at their worst, is always at the height which this human nature can attain.

In making this decision as to which self is the real self, we have to distinguish clearly between our animal nature and our human nature. Some years ago the eminent scientist George Dorsey wrote a learned book entitled *Why We Behave Like Human Beings.* One reviewer said, "The answer is plain. Most of us don't." As we think of our grim and brutal age, it is easy to shrug our shoulders and say, "What can you expect of human nature?" We protest! We simply are *not* behaving like human beings. Man often acts like an animal —more often than not with apologies to the animal—but it is *man* acting like an animal. When he does so, he is not revealing his real nature but betraying it. Animal nature and human nature are two different things.

Suppose, for example, one saw a big dog mauling a puppy. It would not occur to him to say, "Come, be yourself, be a dog." He is being a dog. If, however, one saw a bully abusing a child, he could say to him, "Be yourself, be a man." An animal acts wholly from instinct. This is why "there is no sin in

45

the farmyard." Man, too, acts from instinct. Biologically he inherits and shares the basic drives of the animal world. These original tendencies are God-given, indispensable, and when wisely directed, invaluable. But to identify man with his primitive drives, as though when you had plumbed the depths of his biological inheritance, there was nothing left to explore, just is not true.

> Man hath all that Nature hath, but more,
> And in that *more* lie all his hopes of good.[2]

It is in that "more" that man finds his uniquely human endowment. He sees visions and dreams dreams. His creative powers find expression in beautiful works of art, inspiring music, ennobling literature. His moral sense, the mark of God on him, lays him under constant obligation to the claims of truth and duty. Though his days are few and fleeting, God has put eternity in his heart, and he faces death with the "lively hope" that beyond its seeming finality are the portals of eternal life. No animal, so far as we know, possesses such gifts or graces. In them is found our uniquely human nature as opposed to our primitive, animal endowment.

To be one's self then, a man has to decide, first of all, on which side of the fence he stands. He does not belong in the pastures or even the barn, but in the house. He is man, not animal. "I remain," says George R. Stewart, speaking as man, "and seem likely to remain, a somewhat altered fish, a slightly remodeled ape." [3] But as Edwin McNeill Poteat comments, "One cannot forbear the observation that never ape, original or remodeled, made an observation like that." [4]

It follows in the second place, that to be one's self involves not only decision, but discipline. It is by disciplining the

---

[2] Matthew Arnold, "To An Independent Preacher."

[3] *Man: An Autobiography* (New York: Random House, 1946), p. 291.

[4] *God Makes the Difference* (New York: Harper & Bros., 1951), p. 55.

lower self, that the best self, the real self, comes into its own. Discipline is never popular. Indeed, there are those to whom it is not only unwanted, but unwarranted. Yet without it self-hood is impossible.

There are three attitudes we may assume towards our body. We may regard our biological inheritance as being wholly good. After all were not our instincts given us by God, and if so, can it be wrong to express them freely? We are ourselves when we obey nature's voice. To be ourselves we need only to do what comes naturally. The voice of conscience, the sense of duty, are artificial restraints which clog the stream of life.

This is indeed a tempting philosophy. The only trouble is that it is a disastrous one. To put our original tendencies in the driver's seat, let ourselves go, act as if our moral sense were an illegitimate child to be abandoned, or an erratic compass whose pointings we can ignore with impunity, is to engage in the fatal act of self-deception. The philosophy which says, "Do what you feel like doing, when you feel like it," means the deterioration of true selfhood. From the day that the first prodigal started for the far country to the end of time, it will remain true that that road leads to disaster. It denies or betrays the deepest truth about man: his spiritual nature.

A second possible view of our body is that which regards it, not as wholly good, but as wholly evil. The body with its urges and drives is something vile and base, an enemy to be slain. The monastic movement was largely built on this idea of mortifying the flesh. It did not accomplish its end. To torture our bodies, as though there was something meritorious in making ourselves miserable, is an unwholesome attitude. If it is wrong to capitulate to nature, it is equally wrong to deny her rightful claims.

The timeless gospel, as I understand it, adopts neither of these positions. It projects a third view. It does not regard our bodies with their instincts and passions as being innately

47

good. Paul tells us that if we are "in the flesh," we cannot please God. Sin, the deadly enemy of our life, reigns in our mortal bodies, and the battle is set. Nor does Christianity regard the flesh as being inherently evil. Indeed, Paul speaks of our bodies as being temples of God. He writes: "Glorify God in your body" (I Cor. 6:20) ; to the Philippians he says, "Christ will be honored in my body." (1:20.) And to the Romans, "I appeal to you . . . brethren, by the mercies of God, to present your bodies as a living sacrifice, holy and acceptable to God, which is your spiritual worship." (12:1.) In a word, the gospel distinguishes between the "natural man," man as a child of nature, and the "spiritual man," man as a child of God. Real selfhood is achieved when by God's grace, our natural impulses become our servants, and not our masters. "Do not yield your members to sin as instruments of wickedness, but yield yourselves to God as men who have been brought from death to life, and your members to God as instruments of righteousness." (Rom. 6:13.) This involves discipline. And why not?

Physical analogies are never wholly adequate in illustrating spiritual truths. Yet our glorification of "nature in the raw" is contradicted every day in experience. Where nature grows weeds, we plant flowers. We convert her waste to wealth, her power to purposes beyond her knowing. This is the key to our progress in science. We speak of our "mastery of nature." The secret of this mastery is our refusal to accept the limitations nature imposes. It is not natural for steel to float or for objects heavier than air to remain aloft. It is not natural for a man to speak in his home and be heard thousands of miles away; not natural for him to sit before a screen and see events transpiring beyond the range of ordinary sight. Left to herself, nature would not have accomplished any of these feats. She has put definite limits to the range of our voice, our ears, our eyes. Yet we have immeasurably extended these limits, surmounted these natural barriers to freedom. This is because, though man is a child of nature, he transcends nature. He imposes on nature his creative intelligence and disciplined effort. This is the mark of his unique selfhood, an indication of the image of the Eternal within him.

Herein lies the crux of the human problem. The tragedy of man lies in this, that while he refuses to accept "nature in the raw," when he deals with the world without, he is for the most part unwilling to impose on his own nature the very disciplined, purposeful effort that has made "the desert rejoice and blossom as a rose." (Isa. 35:1 K.J.V.) This is why our mechanical progress has so far outdistanced our spiritual growth. Scientifically we are giants, spiritually pigmies. But progress is not measured by the skill with which we release or manipulate the powers of nature, but rather by the control we have over our own. "He who is slow to anger is better than the mighty, and he who rules his spirit than he who takes a city." (Prov. 16:32.) Indeed, it is only as we learn to rule our spirits that our cities, if not our world, can be saved from destruction. Discipline then is an indispensable step on the road to true selfhood.

But consider now a third step. In some respects this is the most important of all. For essential as are decision and discipline, they are not enough. To these we must add dedication—commitment to the highest and best we know. As the late Archbishop of Canterbury, William Temple, writes:

What is quite certain is that the self cannot by any effort of its own lift itself off its own self as centre. . . Such radical conversion must be the act of God, . . . Nothing can suffice but a redemptive act. Something impinging upon the self from without must deliver it from the freedom which is perfect bondage to the bondage which is its only perfect freedom.[5]

[5] *Nature, Man and God* (London: Macmillan & Co. Ltd., 1935), p. 397.

This I think does not mean that sincere efforts at self-improvement are to be dismissed as being without significance or value. Yet the fact is that the self cannot be itself by itself. We cannot lift ourselves by our boot straps. Selfhood is achieved by commitment to that which is above and beyond the self. By our reason we can decide who we are. By our wills we can discipline ourselves. But our wills are weak! "To will is present with me; but how to perform that which is good I find not." (Rom. 7:18 K.J.V.) Commitment to God achieves what neither reason nor will, invaluable though they be, can provide. It brings the thought life, the emotional life, and the imagination under God's control. In these areas are the decisive forces of our life.

Consider an orchestra. Before the concert begins, the players stroll indifferently on the stage and take their seats. Each without reference to the others, begins to play some little musical phrase on his particular instrument. The result is bedlam. Presently, however, the conductor appears. Every eye is now centered on him. Each player, no longer fancy-free, co-operates with his fellows. The noise stops. The music begins. The orchestra becomes itself. Why? Because it is now related to that which is outside itself—the will of the conductor as he interprets a beautiful symphony. The players have now found that which unifies and directs.

Our personalities are something like an orchestra in the tuning-up stage. When H. G. Wells says of one of his characters that he is not so much a human being as a civil war, we know what he means. Vagrant desires claim the floor, demanding to be heard. Yet, each of us knows that the satisfaction of a desire does not necessarily mean the satisfaction of a person. On the contrary, it often produces the keenest dissatisfaction. It engulfs us in remorse and regrets. Should these warnings go unheeded, the result may be the deterioration of personality. We need something—more truly someone—to do for us what a conductor does for an orchestra:

bring our divided selves into cohesion and unity. This is the secret of self-mastery. Strangely enough, self-mastery is achieved as the self finds its master. As someone has said, "The search of the scholarly mind is to master something. The quest of the religious mind is to find some masterful thing."

That "masterful thing" may be for some an ennobling friendship or a deep affection; for others a sobering sense of responsibility. Millions down the ages, however, have found it supremely in Christ. "Ye call me Master. . . and ye say well; for so I am." (John 13:13 K.J.V.) Jesus is Master because he himself was so completely mastered by God, to whose will and purpose he was fully committed. The mystery of his life lies in this, that in making God known through our human flesh, he not only revealed God's nature, but also man's true nature. In showing what God is like, he also showed what we potentially are and may become. "Jesus, divinest when thou most art man!" [6] The paradox of Jesus' life is that he is most like man when he is most like God. That is to say, he achieved his real selfhood by the complete commitment of his life to God. To the degree that we make a like commitment, we are on the road to our true selfhood. This is why James Stewart says that sometime or other in his life, every man must kneel before Christ if he is to be fully man.

In the last analysis then, to be one's self is to find that which transcends the self and give one's devotion to this. As we mature, we see more clearly than we did in our younger days that the secret of our strength lies not in what we hold —our grip is weak—but in what holds us; not in what we command, but in what commands us. Paul voiced a great truth when he said, "I have kept the faith" (II Tim. 4:7), but I think Peter revealed a greater one when he spoke of those "who are kept by the power of God through faith."

[6] Frederic W. H. Myers, *Saint Paul* (London: Macmillan & Co., Ltd., 1908), p. 16.

(I Pet. 1:5 K.J.V.) It is through the power of this faith in a God who created us in his image, loves us and through Christ redeems us from the sin which destroys his image, that we grow towards "a perfect man, unto the measure of the stature of the fulness of Christ" (Eph. 4:13 K.J.V.) —Christ, symbol of our real self.

"When he came to himself, he said, . . . I will arise and go to my father." It is as though Christ were saying to each of us, "Be yourself!"

V

How We Come to Know God

". . . the knowledge of God, rather than burnt offerings."
—HOS. 6:6

WE CANNOT BE OURSELVES APART FROM GOD. THE KNOWLedge of God is necessary to the realization of our real selfhood, because the deepest thing in us is God's image in our souls. Augustine voiced this truth when he said, "God is more deeply within me than I am myself." Without God, man is truly "a troubled wanderer upon a darkened earth." If this be true, then no knowledge that we acquire is so important as our knowledge of God, for apart from him all other knowledge is fragmentary, purposeless, and may even become, as is now possible, the means of our destruction. God, speaking through his prophet, said, "For I desire steadfast love and not sacrifice, the knowledge of God, rather than burnt offerings." "Burnt offerings," however, are not the only inadequate substitute. Man being what he is, there is no adequate substitute for the knowledge of God. Let us think then of how we come to know God. Perhaps, first of all, we should clarify the subject by making a few preliminary observations—familiar though they be.

There is a difference between knowing about God and knowing him. Knowing about God is important, but is never the same as knowing him. God is more than a subject of study. He is the object of experience. "It is quite possible," wrote Henry Churchhill King, "to be Christian in head and pagan in heart; to have learned much of theology, and yet to be sadly clear that one stands in no close relation to God himself."[1]

Again. We could not know God had he not, as we have said, put into our hearts something akin to himself. Epictetus was not a Christian, yet how Christian was his insight when he wrote: "But you are a superior thing; you are a portion separated from the deity; you have in yourself a certain portion of him." Our search for God is therefore always a double search. He seeks us more tirelessly and constantly than we seek him. "We love him, because he first loved us." (I John 4:19 K.J.V.) Our desire to know him and our capacity to do so are gifts from him. But for this, none of us could know him.

None of us can know God completely, since he is infinite and we finite. As Augustine puts it, "If thou couldst comprehend Him He would not be God," or in the words of a saintly rabbi, "If you were to understand Him you would be God." Such statements corroborate one of the deep insights of the Bible. Job asks, "Can you find out the deep things of God? Can you find out the limit of the Almighty? It is higher than heaven—what can you do? Deeper than Sheol—what can you know?" (Job 11:7-8.) Why should this disturb us? There is a veil of mystery that surrounds our life. We see through a glass darkly. Do we know each other completely, or even ourselves? We can "apprehend," though never fully "comprehend" the Eternal, whose ways, as Paul says, are "past finding out." As a matter of fact, a God whom we completely knew would be of little value to us since he would be no greater than ourselves. We should then lose the incentive to grow in grace and in the knowledge and love of God.

Once more. Not all of us find God by the same road. John says there are twelve gates to the city. We may not all use the same gate. Some of us are more mystical than practical. Some are imaginative and sensitive, others less so.

[1] *Greatness and Simplicity of the Christian Faith* (Nashville: Tidings), p. 39.

Let us then mention, of necessity in barest outline, some of the ways in which men become aware of God.

Surely one way is through beauty. This approach is more akin to the Greek than the Hebrew tradition. The Hebrew prophets approached God through righteousness, the Greek philosophers through beauty. As the well-known epigram has it, the Greeks worshiped the holiness of beauty, the Hebrews the beauty of holiness. The Hebrew prophets were right, but the Greek philosophers were not wrong. There is something eternal in beauty.

A concert by the late Sergei Rachmaninoff stands out most vividly in my memory. No one could have convinced me at its close that I had only heard an ungainly looking man playing a piano. God spoke through that recital. The artist was the medium through which one caught the overtone of something eternally significant. So God speaks through great music, literature, art, and the splendor of nature. Studdert-Kennedy said that whenever he was tempted to doubt the goodness of God, the first challenge he had to meet was the sheer beauty of God's world. "The longer I live," he wrote, "the more it means to me. When my soul gives up the fight for faith and tries to sneer at life, God hoists again the flags of dawn, or blows his trumpet from the hills, and brings me humbly back again." [2]

Valid, however, as is this approach, it is not in and of itself adequate. Many people who adore beauty may do so without seeing in it the garment of God. Whenever one sees God in beauty, he has first found him within his own soul. The psalmist could say, "The heavens declare the glory of God" (Ps. 19:1 K.J.V.), but for others they may declare only the purposeless rumbling of unconscious power. If, like the Master, one sees God in the sunset, the lilies of the field, or

[2] *The Word and the Work* (New York: Longmans, Green & Co., Inc. 1925), p. 7.

the face of a child, it is because he has first found him elsewhere.

We are sometimes made aware of God in the crises of life, when deep calls unto deep. The crisis may be one of imminent danger. We have heard much in recent years of "foxhole religion." Men facing danger or death adrift in rubber rafts on the pitiless ocean instinctively pray. Now, let us admit that such turning to God, when we are at our wit's end, is by no means the highest expression of faith. Yet it is a significant expression. Religion has been defined as "the feeling of absolute dependence." So in imminent danger the garment of our imagined self-sufficiency falls from us, and in our helplessness we seek God's help. "I hadn't prayed in ten years," a railroad man exclaimed when his train narrowly escaped a wreck, "but I prayed *then.*"

Sometimes the crisis is induced by grief in one of its many forms. I knew a mother who thus found God. Her son, a child of six years, died. He had been more than life to her. She was so distraught that she could not go to the cemetery, but stood and watched the funeral procession until it moved out of sight. Then she turned away to face, as she said, either black despair or victorious faith. She found God. So did Harry Lauder. When news reached him that his only son had been killed in battle, he said to a friend who came to sympathize:

I have had my moments of bitterness and desolation. I have been at the point when a man does one of three things—he becomes desperate, or takes to drink, or turns to God. John, I have had to turn to God, the God we learnt about when we were lads together. Let's kneel down and pray as we used to in the Auld Kirk.[3]

The crisis may be induced by some great responsibility

[3] Stanley I. Stuber and Thomas Curtis Clark, *Treasury of the Christian Faith* (New York: Association Press, 1949), p. 292.

to which we feel unequal. When Lincoln was leaving Spring-field, Illinois, to assume the burdens of the presidency, he said in his farewell address:

> I now leave, not knowing when, or whether ever, I may return, with a task before me greater than that which rested upon Washington. Without the assistance of that Divine Being who ever attended him I cannot succeed. With that assistance I cannot fail.[4]

One ventures that in these troubled times, when the outlook is ominous, more people are trying the uplook than heretofore. "In the year that King Uzziah died I saw the Lord." (Isa. 6:1.) Uzziah was one of Israel's great kings. His death brought on a national crisis. As his nation's destiny hung in the balance, Isaiah became more vividly aware of God—"I saw the Lord." Even so, the problems we confront and their attendant perils are of such terrifying proportions that we are becoming increasingly aware of the inadequacy of our wisdom, power, or ingenuity to solve them. We are aware of our insufficiency and so of God.

> I will lift up my eyes to the hills.
>> From whence does my help come?
> My help comes from the Lord,
>> Who made heaven and earth. (Ps. 121:1-2.)

Most important of all, the crisis may be a moral one. Like the Prodigal in some far country, we suddenly awaken to the fact that we have missed the way. We see ourselves as we are, and then think of what we might be. We realize, as did the Prodigal, that the bread of evil never satisfies, but only increases our hunger. We eat and yet are starved. We feed yet are never filled. We are satiated but not satisfied. We go from one thrill to another until disillusionment leads to dis-

[4] *Ibid.*, p. 291.

gust. Then we come to ourself, our real self. "How many of my father's hired servants have bread enough and to spare, but I perish here with hunger! I will arise and go to my father." (Luke 15:17-18.) His physical hunger was only a part of it. The real hunger was the hunger of his soul for decency and true selfhood. In all such soul-searching experiences God is near, offering pardon to the penitent and the hope of renewed fellowship.

So through beauty, through the crises of life induced by danger, suffering, sobering responsibility, or sin, God is made known to us.

But, of course, we have not yet mentioned what for countless souls is the surest path to God. It is the road blazed by One who said, "I am the way." (John 14:6.) Indeed there are those who may think that all we have said so far is inconsequential. It is as though we have been lighting little candles and ignoring the sun which makes their flickering flame unnecessary. This, however, is not so. For beauty and life's recurring crises are an inseparable part of God's disclosure of himself in Christ.

If beauty is not a valid part of God's revelation in Christ, how can one account for the fact that Christianity has inspired some of the most priceless possessions of our culture —as seen in beautiful architecture, music, painting, and the like? Or why is it that at Christmas, when we commemorate Christ's birth, everything seems to take on added beauty—our homes, our churches, even our commercial buildings are less drab and colorless. No wonder they are. For whether we sing about the Babe in the manger, the shepherds in the field, the wise men with their gifts, or the star, we seem to see them all through the glory of the Lord that shone about them. Even we ourselves do not escape. We are more likely to smile than frown. Our customary preoccupation with self gives way to gracious thoughts and deeds. Beauty is a mark of God. It awakens an awareness of God. It is no coincidence that man began his life in a garden. Ugliness is another word for sin.

And as to the crises of life, these are the key to our understanding of Jesus' ministry. His temptation in the wilderness, which marked the beginning of his public ministry, as his struggle in Gethsemane which marked its close, called for decisions and choices which changed the course of history. In these crucial experiences he confronted his Father, whose will and purpose he sought to fulfill.

While we find in Christ the counterpart of the beauty that stirs our souls and the crises that reveal our dependence, they do not really give us the knowledge we seek. The author of the Epistle to the Hebrews gives us the key to this knowledge:

Therefore, brethren, since we have confidence to enter the sanctuary by the blood of Jesus, by the new and living way which he opened for us through . . . his flesh, . . . let us draw near with a true heart in full assurance of faith. (10:19-22.)

Christ has opened "the new and living way" to God. What is this "new and living way"? Why is it that adown the ages when men have sought their clearest and fullest knowledge of God, they have found this knowledge in Christ? Let us suggest a few reasons.

For one thing, Jesus personalizes our thought of God. Beauty? But could there be beauty without eyes that see it, and hearts that cherish it? And when we speak of the crises of life, we are not speaking of abstractions, but of *men* involved in situations—men thinking, praying, wrestling like Jacob of old, deciding. Persons alone give meaning to this world of ours. Personality is the highest concept we have. Jesus is the "new and living way" to God, because he reveals God to us through the mystery of his personality. This is the meaning of the Incarnation—"God was in Christ" (II Cor. 5:19), as

59

he has never been in anyone before or since. Athanasius, enlarging on this truth, writes:

He takes to Himself as an instrument a part of the whole, the human body, and unites Himself with that, in order that since men . . . could not look up to His invisible power, they might be able at any rate, from what resembled themselves, to reason to Him and to contemplate Him.[5]

In the story of the nativity, the star, symbol of the material universe, leads to a child—personality.

Now when we think of God in terms of personality, we are often accused of anthropomorphism; that is, of making God in our own image. But how else can man think of the Creator, if not in terms of "what resembled themselves"—that is, in terms of the highest concept we have, personality? There are, to be sure, those who in order to escape this charge, think of God as being less than human personality. Haeckel, the materialist, "laughs to scorn the opening clause of the 'Apostles Creed.' 'I believe in God the Father Almighty.' " But what did he believe in? What was his concept of God? "I believe in 'a chemical substance of viscous character, having albuminous matter and water as its chief constituents' " [6] For him the nativity story ends with the star, physical energy, blind force, omnipotent matter. This, no doubt, avoids the charge of anthropomorphism, but does it not create greater problems?

For what a strange world this would be if it happened that some impersonal power had somehow managed to produce persons; if that which is lower than man, unknowing, uncaring, purposeless matter, had created that which was

[5] Quoted in John Baillie, "Day 17," *A Diary of Readings* (New York: Charles Scribner's Sons, 1955).

[6] Harry Emerson Fosdick, *The Meaning of Faith* (New York: Association Press, 1919), p. 66.

higher than itself—persons, with minds that think and reason, hearts that love, consciences sensitive to good and evil, heroic spirits capable of the utmost in sacrificial love. We just cannot believe that Haeckel's creed accounts for Christ. However much greater God may be than personal, he cannot be less! Personality is the key to our knowledge of God. And in the *best* personality, in Christ, "the fairest among ten thousand," "the one altogether beautiful," we see God's fullest revelation of himself, and so the path to our surest knowledge of the Eternal. The Christ of the Fourth Gospel says, "He who has seen me has seen the Father" (John 14:9). We share the faith of Paul, who sees "the light of the knowledge of the glory of God in the face of Christ" (II Cor. 4:6).

But in Christ we have our surest knowledge of God, not only because he reveals God through the highest we know, through his personality, but also because he reveals personality in its highest expression—sacrificial, self-giving love, the Cross. But why *his* cross? When one thinks of the millions of crosses that cover the earth, the question naturally arises, "What is there about the cross on Calvary that gives it such timeless significance? Why has the most degraded symbol of the ancient world become for millions the world over their most honored and revered symbol? There is only one adequate answer to that question. It is found in God's revelation of himself through the personality of Jesus—in theological language, the incarnation of God in Christ. If the cross of Jesus has been for millions down the ages the word of God to their souls, the key to their fullest knowledge of him, it is because Calvary was not an affair between men, not the occasion on which evil men crucified a good man, but the God-man. Apart from that faith, our reverence for the Cross, the power it has had through the ages until now, has been sadly misplaced. It would be hard to believe that.

61

But granting that God was in Christ, why, one may still ask, should the Cross be the key to our fullest knowledge of God? Why not Jesus preaching on the mount to the multitudes, or blessing little children, or healing the sick? Why choose his death rather than some incident from his life as the truest revelation of God? Is this the answer—that, in the Cross, as nowhere else, we see three truths. We see the sad truth about ourselves. The Cross shows the depth of our alienation from God, the sin that separates us so far from him that it led men, in Paul's words, to crucify the Lord of glory. We see, too, the extent to which God goes in removing the barrier between himself and his children. He spared not his own son. In other words, He gave himself. And, finally, we see that the death of Jesus, which men thought would be the end of him, actually proved to be the beginning of his world-wide ministry. The darkness that fell on Calvary proved to be the darkest hour before the dawn. Easter is testimony to the *victory* of God over sin and death, the triumph of God's power and love over the very worst that man can do. That victory has opened a door which no man can shut—the door to renewed fellowship with the God and Father of our Lord, Jesus Christ, the God of our salvation. John Hutton summarizes what we have been saying better than we can say it: "You cannot understand the mystery of the universe without God; you cannot understand the mystery of God without Christ; and you cannot understand the mystery of Christ without the Cross." [7]

And so for our truest knowledge of God we look to him, the "new and living way." Through beauty or the recurring crises of our experiences, we may be aware of God. But it is through Christ that we come to know the true nature of "a presence that disturbs . . . with the joy of elevated

[7] Frank H. Caldwell, *Preaching Angles* (New York and Nashville: Abingdon Press, 1954), p. 119.

thoughts." Whenever God becomes for us "the Lost Word," that word is found again in the Word that became flesh.

For he is our peace, who has made us both one, and has broken down the dividing wall of hostility, . . . that he . . . might reconcile us both to God in one body through the cross, thereby bringing the hostility to the end. (Eph. 2:14-16.)

VI

What Prayer Can Do for Us

*"Search me, O God, and know my heart: try me
and know my thoughts: and see if there be any
wicked way in me, and lead me in the way everlasting."*
                                              —PS. 139:23

WHEN WE COME TO KNOW GOD, WE DO NOT SIMPLY TALK
about him, we speak to him. He is not just an abstract, vague
idea with which our minds toy, but becomes a living Presence
with whom our souls commune. So deeply ingrained is the
impulse to pray, that sometimes, even though God be an "An
Unknown God," like the Athenians of old, we build altars
to him, and make gestures of adoration or supplication in his
direction.

Instead of discussing prayer in the abstract, let us center
our thoughts about a concrete example of it. The fact that
the prayer we shall consider was voiced long ago, centuries
before the birth of Christ, yet is still so relevant to our needs
today, shows that in speaking of prayer, we are dealing with
something of enduring value. Prays the psalmist, "Search me,
O God, and know my heart: try me, and know my thoughts:
And see if there be any wicked way in me, and lead me in the
way everlasting."

We can see immediately one of the limitations of this ut-
terance. It seemingly lacks social vision, social concern. There
is not in it the horizons of "Thy kingdom come," or even
of, "Give *us* this day our daily bread." Yet it is the sincere ut-

terance of one conscious of his creaturehood, his limitations, and his sin.

The first thing about this old prayer that gives it religious significance is that it is quite personal. It begins with *me:* "Search me, O God." We may justly criticize the psalmist for stopping there, but we cannot criticize him for starting there, for that is where all genuine prayer begins—in the personal communion of the soul with God. When we study astronomy, we begin with the stars; geology, with the rocks; and music, with the scales; but, when we move into the realm of religion, we really do not get to the heart of the matter until we get to ourselves. "Search me, O God." Without that, there could be no prayer. "He that cometh to God must believe that he is, and that he is a rewarder of them that diligently seek him." (Heb. 11:6 K.J.V.) Back of all prayer lies, first of all, a genuine belief in a God who is interested in us, knows and loves us. It is incredible that men would have continued praying adown the ages until now, if they had thought they were merely talking to themselves. It is incredible that prayer would have survived if men honestly believed that they were only "improving the quality of their own voice." Men pray, as this psalmist did, because they believe someone hears them —someone with whom they come into personal relationship. ship.

There are many things, no doubt, that make it difficult for modern man to believe in this personal relationship between his soul and God.

One set of difficulties comes from the scientific world. The very immensity of the universe that modern science has revealed, tends "to choke our prayers." "When I consider thy heavens, . . . What is man?" (Ps. 8:3, 4.) Yet how relatively small was his universe compared with ours with its billions of light years. Again, the psalmist lived in a world which was not so fully aware of the workings of natural law as is ours. God was frequently thought of as one who would, through miraculous intervention, interrupt the orderly processes of nature to grant the requests of his children.

Once more. Many of the things for which men in a pre-scientific age prayed seem now to be obtained through man's resourcefulness and ingenuity. Modern science has delivered man from many hardships and limitations which previously made him aware of his dependence on God.

The scientific method freed man from immemorial limitations. It gave him a sharp, hard tool for cutting into the rock-faced situations of his world where he had formerly banged with his fists and mumbled incantations. It transformed him from a suppliant into a god.[1]

So now if one is ill, a skilled physician, not God, is his need. If he is mentally distressed, a psychiatrist, not God, is his answer. If he is in need, some social agency, not the Most High, is his recourse. So some seem to think!

But surely this is shallow thinking. As if the most skilled technique could answer the deepest cry of man's spirit, or meet his profoundest need. The plain truth is that, in spite of it all, men still pray. It is interesting to discover that not from the Church alone, but from some of our most reputable scientific men are now coming testimonies as to the importance and reality of prayer. Alexis Carrel writes:

Prayer is a force as real as terrestrial gravity. As a physician, I have seen men, after all other therapy had failed, lifted out of disease and melancholy by the serene effort of prayer. It is the only power in the world that seems to overcome the so-called laws of nature; the occasions on which prayer has dramatically done this have been termed "miracles." But a constant, quieter miracle takes place hourly in the hearts of men and women who have

[1] Hugh Stevenson Tigner, *Our Prodigal Son Culture* (Chicago and New York: Willett, Clark & Co., 1940), p. 99.

discovered that prayer supplies them with a steady flow of sustaining power in their daily lives.[2]

This is a reassuring word, and Carrel's is no lone voice. He feels, as do others qualified to speak, that nothing that has happened in the scientific world has made impossible the communion of man's spirit with God.

There is another source of difficulty. And it springs not from science, but from within ourselves. Quite often the trouble lies not with science, but with us. We may profess to believe in God and even pray to him, yet all the while we are haunted by the sense of unreality. We repeat the familiar words of Tennyson:

> Speak to Him, thou, for He hears, and
> Spirit with Spirit can meet—
> Closer is He than breathing, and
> nearer than hands and feet.[3]

But we wonder if God really hears, and if he is as near as the poet makes out.

What does one do when God seems unreal? We should realize for one thing that these dry seasons of the soul come to all of us. They are as old as prayer itself. Job cried: "Oh, that I knew where I might find him" (Job 23:3.) The prophet speaks of God as one who hideth himself: "Then shall they cry unto the Lord, but he will not hear them: he will even hide his face from them." (Mic. 3:4 K.J.V.) Yet we must remember that even on the darkest day when the sun is hidden from our sight, it is still shining—shining though we cannot see it. Jesus told his disciples a parable "to the effect that they ought always to pray and not lose heart" (Luke 18:1). "Always"— when we feel like it and when we do not, when God seems

[2] *Reader's Digest*, March, 1941, p. 34.
[3] "The Higher Pantheism."

real and when he does not; remembering that God is always "there," despite our changing moods.

We should remember, too, that more often than not these clouds are of our own making. In every great experience of life there are always certain conditions that must be met ere we distill their rich meaning. A man who walks patronizingly through an art gallery, casting a hurried glance here and there, would hardly be a judge of its worth, any more than would one undisciplined in the art of listening to great music, be regarded as a competent critic in such matters. Surely it cannot be otherwise with prayer. One basic condition here is sincerity of purpose. One soon learns that there is a difference between saying one's prayers, and praying. "Saying our prayers" can be a matter of words. Praying sincerely is a matter of life. We soon discover how futile it is to send our words in one direction and our life in another. Prayer is not giving God lip service, but life service. The story has it that a little girl who could not break the habit of eating green apples was advised by her mother to pray about it. She did. But that night her mother found a green apple under her pillow!

> My words fly up, my thoughts remain
> below:
> Words without thoughts never to
> heaven go.[4]

If, therefore, one says of prayer, "There is nothing in it for me," that surely does not mean that there is nothing in it. It might only mean that he has not met one of the basic requirements—sincerity. One might say of prayer what the guard said to the the tourist who could see nothing of interest in a European art gallery: "Madam, these pictures are not on trial, you are."

[4] William Shakespeare, *Hamlet,* Act. III, Scene 3.

Another thing that helps us when prayer seems unreal, is the simple act of recalling the moments when it was real, when we were conscious of God's presence and grace—and who of us has not had such moments? Who of us, like Moses, has not at some time met God by some burning bush; or like Elijah, has not at some time heard the still small voice; or like Jacob on his pilgrimage, felt that the Lord was in this place. No one has a copyright on the experience of God. He may enter your life through one door, and mine by another. The seer of Revelation with true insight saw twelve gates to the city. Not all of us use the same one.

In those moments then when God may seem remote or unreal, we may call to mind the times when he was real. Ignatius said, "He who hath heard the Word of God can bear his silences." Indeed, a man's spiritual life is somewhat like a stretch of railroad on the northern shore of Jamaica. Within a distance of some thirty or forty miles there are ten or more tunnels. You travel along the shore line with the blue sea beside and a bright sky above, and suddenly it is dark. But a tunnel, remember, has light at both ends. So a man when he passes through the shadows tries to remember the moments of unsullied vision.

This then, is one thing we may learn from this old prayer— that neither the alleged difficulties of our scientific age, nor our own ineptitude or moods or tempers, need make us doubt the validity and reality of the personal communion of our spirit with the Eternal Spirit.

In the second place, observe the things for which the psalmist prays, the area in which his thought moves. He does not pray for material blessings, but for spiritual strength and illumination. "Search me—Try me—Lead me." Some of us who have given up the practice of prayer have done so, I fancy, because we have outgrown the crude ideas we once had of it, and have not moved on to discover its deeper values or meaning. Too many people have regarded God as a sort of cosmic engineer who in response to their petition would, on short notice, throw a monkey wrench into the machinery of his universe, in order to grant some personal wish of theirs. Lin Yutang holds up to ridicule, and justly I think, a Christian relative of his who, thought she had through prayer, stopped a four-day rain in Changchow so that his mother might be buried in the sunshine.

We are not prepared to say that we should never pray about material things; yet it is true that the psalmist, in turning to the unseen world—the world of motive and of purpose—was touching a vastly more important realm than the material. To him, prayer was the means of bringing his hidden inner life under the light of the Eternal. Would anyone doubt that, by all odds, this inner world is by far the most decisive area of life? Is there anything that ever happens out there—in the world we see and touch—that has not had its inception in the inner hidden world? Plato taught that the real world was the world of ideas, and that all visible things were in reality only shadows cast by the invisible realities. He would have endorsed the words of Paul, that the things not seen are eternal. The real man is the man we never see; and it is in this area of the unseen that the psalmist invokes the searching light of the Eternal.

Who can doubt the truth of his analysis? Consider the world in which we live. We are masters of the world; but because we are not masters of ourselves, we are being mastered by the world, as the things which we produce or invent —proud offspring of our unrepentant hearts and unregenerate thoughts—are being used for our destruction. It is hard to see how anyone can doubt today the primacy of the spiritual world, for has not our faith in the material world failed us? We are pinning our faith now on the power of material things to safeguard our civilization. During World War II, before we entered it, Mr. Churchill said, "Give us the tools and we will finish the job." We gave him the tools, but they did not finish the job. Since then we have devised more terrible tools, vastly more destructive than even Mr. Churchill then imagined. But these will not finish the job, though indeed they may finish us. Planes, ships, and hydrogen bombs will never stop wars any more than they start wars. Wars will be stopped when the inner world, the world of motive, purpose, and desire, is oriented Godward.

We say this is idealism. What do we mean when we say that? Is it not sheer common sense? For is it not now evident that we never really change the world without until we change the world within? It is the inner world which man seems powerless to change through his resolution or even his good intentions. How admirable have been our intentions, but how inadequate. The League of Nations was a good intention. Theoretically it could have established a world of international justice, security, and peace. The Kellogg-Briand Pact for the outlawing of war was another good intention. It could have made war as obsolete a method for settling disputes between nations as dueling now is between civilized men. The United Nations is a good intention. It is potentially capable of creating an international community of law-abiding peoples. Yet, how well we now know that these marvelous blueprints of a better world are only scraps of paper unless they are infused with the spirit of good will, co-operation and trust. This is the tragic lot of man—that he knows so much better than he does, he sees so much farther than he can go. We are not criticizing such efforts as we make. Far from it. They are necessary. We are merely trying to point out how inadequate they are unless backed up and supported by the deep, unseen urges of man's heart.

It is precisely here that this old prayer brings its timely and timeless message. It brings us to the root of the matter. It calls for nothing less than the submitting of our inner human motives, purposes, thoughts, to the cleansing and redeeming power of God. This is painful spiritual surgery. It

requires a humble, repentant attitude; and humility and repentance are not modern virtues. Yet what but a change within the inner life of man can save us from these ever-recurring
hells; and what can effect that change save the transforming
power of God made available for us through Christ? From
this point of view, you may see how naïve it is to belittle the
importance of prayer. Rather, is it not naïve to try to get on
without it?

Finally, see in this old prayer man's age-old longing for
eternal and timeless values: "Lead me in the way everlasting"
(Ps. 139:24). What is "the way everlasting"? Is it not the
way of God's will? When Jesus in Gethsemane prayed, "Not
as I will, but as thou wilt" (Matt. 25:39), was he not seeking
the way everlasting?

Broadly speaking, it may be said that there are two kinds
of people in the world: those who know nothing higher than
their desires, their will, and those who believe that "God's
will is inherent in every human situation"; those who regard
their own purposes as being ultimate, and those who believe
that God is working out an eternal purpose, and calls them
to find and share in it.

Perhaps an illustration might help. Suppose we are standing on a high building looking down at the moving traffic—
pedestrians hurrying along on the sidewalks, cars going hither
and yon. Each person, each car, is on some mission, going
somewhere that seems important or desirable. But, now suppose we should think not just of the individual pedestrian or
car, this complex of individual wishes and plans, but rather
of all of them together. Where is the group, in its entirety,
going? Does the total movement make sense? Is there any
universal, transcendent purpose that broods over all, within
which finite purposes move, and to which they can be adjusted? Is there some dimension to life that transcends the
level of our own wishes, will, or desires? The Christian faith
asserts that there is.

Yet I doubt not thro' the ages one increasing purpose runs,
And the thoughts of men are widen'd with the process of the
  suns.[5]

To find God's will is not easy. It has been called the most
"precious" and "poignant" element of faith. But it is God's
will that we should seek his will. He who seeks "the way everlasting" lives in tune with the infinite, walks not the calcu-
lating path of expediency, but the adventurous path of faith;
and lives his earthly life in the larger light of the eternal
purpose.

I wonder if the psalmist, in bringing to God his heart, his
thoughts, and seeking the eternal way, did not uncover three
of the imponderables in which men are made aware of God:
the unseen, the silent, the timeless. In our best moments we
feel that we are greater than our bodies. The essential part of
us is that hidden from mortal eyes. In the silent realm of
thought we sense a power so much greater than the clamor
of our noisy world. In the presence of the fleeting and transient we grope for that sense of permanency, enduringness, in
which is the only security for ourselves, or the values we
cherish. As we sense all this, realizing our finitude, we turn
our thoughts as did the psalmist to the Eternal God, and with
him pray, "Search me . . . try me . . . lead me."

[5] Alfred Lord Tennyson, "Locksley Hall," l. 137.

VII

A Thankful Heart

"Were not ten cleansed? Where are the nine?"
—LUKE 17:17

WE ARE PRONE TO THINK OF PRAYER, TOO MUCH PERHAPS, as petition. We voice our needs and ask God to supply them. Often, however, we fail to express our gratitude for what we have received. Let us think then of prayer as thanksgiving.

When one stops to think about the matter, there is little you or I can give to God. For since we believe that God is the Creator of all things visible and invisible, it follows that in making any gift to him, we are only returning a part of what he has given us. For instance, we say we will give him of our time. But time is not ours to give. We only give back to him a portion of the threescore years and ten, more or less, of our allotted span. If we give him of our substance, is it really *our* substance? "The silver is mine, and the gold is mine, says the Lord of hosts." (Hag. 2:8.)

To some, this may seem a strange way of looking at the matter. But is it not true? That it is, may be seen in the fact that we brought nothing into the world and carry nothing out. Since we come into the world with empty hands and leave it as we came, does it not follow that what we have is not really ours? Our life, as our substance, is loaned us as we come, and taken from us as we leave. The question then is whether there is *any* offering we can make, that, in some sense at least, may be regarded as our very own. One of the church fathers, Clement of Alexandria, said that there was only one offering we could make—a thankful heart.

A New Testament story reveals a man with such a heart. Ten lepers, we are told, were healed by Jesus, but only one of them returned to say "thank you." Jesus asked: "Were not ten cleansed? Where are the nine?" It would be interesting to know where they were, or why they did not return. However, we are more concerned about the one who came back to give thanks than with the nine who did not. Let us look at this man and see what kind of heart a thankful heart really is.

For one thing a thankful heart is a thoughtful heart. It is no coincidence that the word "thank" comes from the same root as the word "think." When we are thankless, we are thoughtless. This fact is often seen in children. You give your child something; he takes the gift and starts to walk away. "What do you say?" you ask him. Then comes the subdued and hardly audible, "thank you." We have to teach children to say "thank you" because they are immature. One glaring defect of the immature is thoughtlessness. From this New Testament story it would appear that children are not alone in this regard. Nine of these adults were thoughtless—only one of them returned to express the gratitude which all of them no doubt to some degree may have felt.

But a thoughtful man goes further than that. He realizes not only that gratitude should be expressed, but understands also that it can only be expressed to a person. Cicero regarded gratitude as the mother of all the virtues, but without God gratitude would die, since there would be no one to whom it could be expressed. For while we can be thankful *for* something, we can never be thankful *to* something—only to someone. We can be thankful for our gifts, but only to a giver. This man, we are told, came back praising God, and knelt at Jesus' feet, giving thanks to him. The wire along which gratitude travels, begins with personality and ends with personality. This very feeling of gratitude, then, is in itself a strong argument for the reality of God.

This is where many who profess not to believe in God, yet may feel a sense of inner gratitude, meet an impasse. Some years ago John Baillie of Edinburgh attended a meeting led by a well-known humanist, who professed not to believe in God. He says there was only one prayer in the service, and it was very much like an ordinary liturgical prayer of thanksgiving, except that each phrase where we would ordinarily say, "We thank Thee, O God," was introduced rather with the words, "We are thankful." But that was a dead giveaway. As Baillie suggests, had they said, "We rejoice," they could indeed have left God out. But no one can say, "We are thankful," without acknowledging God's reality. For the question at once arises: thankful to whom?

Leslie Stephen professed not to believe in God. When his wife died, he was deeply affected and wrote to a friend, "I thank —— that I ever knew her." He was about to write the word "God" but since he professed not to believe in him, he sent the letter with his thanks to a blank. We often have occasion to thank each other. But a gratitude that begins in me and ends in you just is not enough. We are but the transient recipients of that which antedates our coming and will continue after we have gone. "They will perish, but thou remainest; . . . like a mantle thou wilt roll them up, and they will be changed." (Heb. 1:11, 12.) "From everlasting to everlasting thou art God." (Ps. 90:2.) God is the only adequate recipient of our gratitude. Without him gratitude would die away.

The thankful heart then is the thoughtful heart. This man who returned not only realized that gratitude should be expressed, but that it could only be expressed to someone, and that someone, God, since he is the ultimate source of all good.

But, once more, a thankful heart is an appreciative heart.

The man who returned had caught the spirit of the one who wrote: "Bless the Lord, O my soul, and forget not all his benefits" (Ps. 103:2). Gratitude springs from some appreciation of God's goodness to us.

Now, what is it that blunts the edge of appreciation? Many things, perchance. Two of them we mention. Surely one thing is the misfortunes, heartaches, and hardships that life brings to many of us. When the psalmist tells us to forget not all God's benefits, he does not mean to say that life is made up entirely of benefits. It is not! There is a debit sheet as well as a credit sheet. If the psalmist urged us to forget not all God's benefits, he must have known that we are more prone to remember our hardships than our benefits, the black-letter days than the red-letter ones. I sometimes think that we lose something in not singing the old gospel songs. Some of them are very good. Do you remember the one that says:

> When upon life's billows you are tempest-tossed,
> When you are discouraged, thinking all is lost,
> Count your many blessings, name them one by one.
> And it will surprise you what the Lord hath done.[1]

This man who came back to give thanks, certainly must have had his fill of black-letter days. He was a leper. When I read recently of how Robert Louis Stevenson, in visiting a leper colony once, shook hands with the lepers and even accepted a gift from one of them, I shuddered. Leprosy is surely one of life's greatest misfortunes. But even this curse had not dulled the edge of appreciation. This leper returned to give thanks. "It is a safe guess that the Samaritan leper was grateful for some things even in his leprosy; only so could he have been grateful for the cure." [2]

[1] Rev. Johnson Oatman, Jr.
[2] *Interpreter's Bible* (New York and Nashville, Abingdon Press, 1952), VIII, 299.

As a matter of fact, clouds and misfortunes, as well as sunshine and blessings can evoke gratitude. To this, the New Testament bears eloquent testimony. Life for the early Christians was no bed of roses. Indeed, their way was more often than not beset with thorns rather than flowers. But they never allowed misfortune to dull the edge of their appreciation. Despite their misfortunes, we hear them saying, "Give thanks in all circumstances" (I Thess. 5:18) and, "Thanks be to God, who gives us the victory through our Lord Jesus Christ" (I Cor. 15:57). And they might have added, "Our Lord Jesus Christ who took the cup of misfortune, and gave thanks."

Consider this stirring hymn:

> Now thank we all our God
>   With heart and hands and voices,
> Who wondrous things hath done,
>   In whom His world rejoices;
> Who, from our mothers' arms,
>   Hath blessed us on our way
> With countless gifts of love,
>   And still is ours today.

Surely that hymn must have been written under cloudless skies, in the blaze of the noonday sun. Ah, but not so! Just the opposite was the case. It was actually written "after a war, famine and pestilence." It was written "by a minister (Martin Rinkart) who had buried so many victims of the plague that by the world's test he should himself have fallen victim to morbidness." [3] But not so. Misfortune had not shaken his faith in the eternal goodness: "Now thank we all our God." Let this leper who returned to give thanks teach us that no day is so dark, no experience so crushing, but that we may appreciate God's goodness to us, and so be grateful. Let us

[3] *Ibid.*

not allow the dark days to obscure the bright ones, and so extinguish the glow of our appreciation, and thus of gratitude. "Forget not all his benefits."

The other condition which kills appreciation is just the opposite—not the misfortunes of life, but its successes, its blessings. To put it bluntly, it often happens that the most ungrateful people on earth are those who have most reason to be grateful. The edge of appreciation, and so of gratitude, is more often dulled by having too many blessings than by not having enough. I am confident, for example, that Lazarus, the beggar, who sat at Dives' gate was much more capable of gratitude than Dives, the rich man, who lived sumptuously.

It is here that this one man who returned has an advantage over us as far as gratitude is concerned. Jesus refers to him as a foreigner. He was a Samaritan, and so was regarded by Jesus' contemporaries as an outcast. He was one of the underprivileged. Is that why he was grateful?

This strange fact comes home to me each summer that I visit Jamaica. I am always impressed with the appreciation the natives—many of whom are poor—express for whatever little help, one may be able to give them. And I have often said to myself, "Am I, relatively prosperous, as appreciative of what others may do for me?" There is sober truth in the remark of Charles Dickens' Mark Tapley, "My not knowing at one meal where I shall get the next is a great help to thankfulness." [4]

Herein lies one of the great differences between our Pilgrim fathers and ourselves. Judged by our standards, they had precious little for which to be grateful. Their food was simple, their shelter of the crudest sort. They faced daily hardships that demanded, at times, the utmost in courage and endurance. The things which we have come to regard as necessities, they would have considered luxuries—if indeed they could

[4] *Martin Chuzzlewit.*

have imagined them. Yet, despite hardships and privations they were genuinely grateful. We, on the contrary, who have so much, whose cup in comparison runneth over, often show little gratitude. We tend to take it all for granted. When we gather for our yearly Thanksgiving services, one wonders at times how genuine it all is. One wonders whether while formally we give thanks to God, behind our professed gratitude there may not lurk the spirit of self-congratulation; as though we ought to thank our genius for mass production, our scientific inventions, our technical know-how, rather than the Almighty.

That is the problem most of us face at the Thanksgiving season—the problem of being genuinely appreciative in the midst of plenty. It is easier to be appreciative in relative poverty than in relative plenty. Yet without such appreciation, Thanksgiving Day may indeed become what Elton Trueblood fears it has become—a thing of artificiality, a time when, before going to a football game, we enjoy a bigger dinner than we usually do.

Now there is only one cure for this, and it is found in the third mark of a thankful heart which we mention. For a thankful heart is not only a thoughtful heart and an appreciative heart, it is also a humble heart. This one man who returned, came and knelt at Jesus' feet, giving him thanks. In this gesture of humility he was acknowledging that the blessing he received had come *to* him, not *from* him. He was saying with Paul: "What have you that you did not receive?" (I Cor. 4:7). And the answer is, "Nothing!"

This is what the privileged so often forget. The privileged are more prone to pat themselves on the back in pride than to bend the knee in humility. Incidentally, if God had intended us to pat ourselves on the back, he surely would have made the joints of our arms differently. It is a rather awkward, if not ugly gesture. But it is so simple and easy to bend the knee.

Pride and gratitude do not mix—proud people are rarely grateful.

This is why the truly great are seldom proud, but are usually simple and humble folk. Whenever you and I are tempted to strut, we should remember that the greatest person who ever walked this earth was described as being "gentle and lowly in heart" (Matt. 11:29). "He humbled himself" (Phil. 2:8), "taking the form of a servant" (vs. 7). He "came not to be served but to serve." (Matt. 20:28.) If the truly great are humble, it is because they realize that their talents were given them and their achievements made possible by the help of others.

We speak of the successful businessman as though he were isolated in solitary splendor from the rest of mortals. But what would the successful businessman be without the men who make his products, and the people who buy them? Or the professional man—how could he succeed but for his patients or clients? Or what would the political leader be, but for those who put him in power and keep him there? What would the artist be without his audience? And the successful minister, how helpless he would be but for loyal, faithful members and friends and the continuing grace, forgiveness, and mercy of God.

The thing for which we should be most grateful is that we can be grateful. If gratitude is the mother of all virtues, as Cicero claimed, it is because it reminds us of our dependence on our fellows and most of all on God—the Giver of every good and perfect gift. When success goes to our heads, it is because gratitude has gone out of our hearts. The more successful one is, the more grateful, the more humble, he should be. Only the immature are proud, and "the proud he knoweth afar off" (Ps. 138:6 K.J.V.).

A minister wrote recently of having received two heirlooms. One was a walnut dresser handed down from his great grandmother on his mother's side. The other was some spoons received from his father's aunt in Germany. "These tokens," he writes, "remind me that on both sides of my family disciplined, cultivated, courageous living has gone into my making. . . . I am simply ashamed to boast of my own achievements." [5]

"I am under obligation both to Greeks and to barbarians," said Paul. (Rom. 1:14.) So are we all. Humility, then, can quicken appreciation and so, gratitude even in the midst of plenty, and deliver us from the mistaken notion of our self-sufficiency and so, our pride.

"Were not ten cleansed?" asked Jesus. "Where are the nine?" Well, where are they? Wherever they are, let us hope that we shall not be found among them.

---

[5] Charles H. Heimsath, *Sermons on the Inner Life* (New York and Nashville: Abingdon Press, 1941), p. 87.

VIII

The Strong Man's Need of God

"For when I am weak, then I am strong."—II COR. 12:10

WHILE IT WOULD BE ADMITTED THAT SOME PEOPLE SEEM to need God and voice their gratitude to him, others seem to get on very well without him. They are quite self-sufficient. Weak people need God, but not strong people; sick people, but not healthy people. People in distress or trouble need God, but not those upon whose paths the sun shines and good fortune smiles. Religion is a sort of crutch for the crippled. But healthy people do not need crutches, they can get along by their own strength, proceed under their own steam.

What shall we say to this opinion? The first observation we make is that since there are so many needy people in the world who have come to the end of their rope, we ought to be glad that this help is available for them at least. Our world is well-nigh bursting at the seams with discouraged people, disheartened people, displaced people, who are at their wit's end. If the gospel is nothing more than a resource for those in trouble, let us be thankful for it. We do live in a troubled world full of troubled people.

We do not as a rule need help in getting into trouble, but most of us need help in getting out of it. If the gospel affords that help let us be grateful that it is available. For it is astonishing what Christianity has done *to* people, *with* people, and *for* people in trouble or need. The Bible bears full testimony to this. "God is our refuge and strength, a very present help in trouble." (Ps. 46:1.) A man who felt privation wrote: "The Lord is my shepherd, I shall not want" (Ps. 23:1). A man who felt his weakness and limitations wrote: "I can do all things in him who strengthens me" (Phil. 4:13). Such statements are typical.

Consider Paul. He stated the matter once in a paradox. Said he, "When I am weak, then I am strong." He had what he called "a thorn . . . in the flesh, a messenger of Satan, to harass me." (II Cor. 12:7.) "I will all the more gladly boast of my weaknesses, that the power of Christ may rest upon me . . . for when I am weak, then I am strong." (vss. 9-19.) Now, I submit that it is much better to be able to say, "When I am weak, then I am strong," than to have to say, "When I am weak, then I am licked." If the Christian religion can take a man like Paul, possessed of some infirmity that threatens his vitality and usefulness, and so empower him, that instead of being broody or embittered, instead of spending his days worrying about his health, feeling his pulse, marooned in the morass of self-pity, he goes forth inspired, undiscouraged, unconquerable, then let us sincerely pray that more people, conscious of their weakness or limitations, will use Christianity as a crutch. There is in religion this power which gives "beauty for ashes, the oil of joy for mourning, the garment of praise for the spirit of heaviness" (Isa. 61:3 K.J.V.).

But now in the second place let us look with a little more discernment at this question of human weakness and strength. Who are the weak? Who are the strong? Here we confront a paradox. The weak often turn out to be the strong; and the strong, the weak. The weak often win out while the strong lose out. It frequently happens that out of human weakness some of the greatest blessings of life have come, while from our alleged strength have come some of the most diabolical and disastrous of life's evils.

Consider human weakness. Is it not true that some of the

very brightest pages of history have been written by those who, like Paul, have had some thorn in the flesh, some conscious limitation or handicap which has threatened to impede, if not quite block their progress? Think of the physically handicapped. It is a familiar fact that Beethoven was so deaf when he wrote some of his greatest works, that he never heard them. It is also true that some of our great artists have had defective eyesight. An astonishing number of the world's great orators have had to overcome, as did Demosthenes, grave speech defects. Immanuel Kant suffered throughout his whole life with a constricted chest that kept him in almost constant pain. But he wrote, "While I felt oppressed in my chest, my head was clear." [1] Such illustrations could be multiplied endlessly. "Would Steinmetz, with his grossly deformed body, have developed his mind to such extraordinary uses had he been an Apollo?" [2]

Now, it will not do to say that such people achieved distinction in spite of their handicaps. It would probably be fairer to say that they achieved because of their handicaps. Adler, the psychologist, says that the greatest human achievements are won at precisely those points where individuals have to struggle most manfully. When Paul said, "When I am weak, then I am strong," he was stating a principle that is widely true. For out of human weakness—accepted, wrestled with and mastered—have come some of life's choicest values. It is an old saying that the poets learn in suffering what they teach in song.

But now consider human strength. It is a curious fact that some of the most disastrous evils that stalk the world—personal and social—come from man's alleged strength. "It is one of the ironies of life that a man's worst calamities result, al-

[1] Quoted in J. H. W. Stuckenberg, *The Life of Immanuel Kant* (London: Macmillan & Co., Ltd., 1882), p. 102.

[2] Harry Emerson Fosdick, *On Being a Real Person* (New York: Harper & Bros., 1943), p. 66.

most always, from his advantages. . . ." [3] They grow not out of his recognized and acknowledged weakness, but out of his supposed strength. If Paul could say, "When I am weak, then I am strong," we could well-nigh say, "Where I am strong, there I am weak."

Take an illustration from the old Edinburgh castle. Only once in the history of Scotland was it ever captured. And this is how it happened. The castle had a weak spot. Defenders guarded that spot. But it was thought that the steepness of the rock on one side of the castle made it inaccessible, impregnable. No sentries were put there. In the gray mist of an early morning an attacking party crept up that strong, unguarded slope and surprised the garrison into surrender. You see, the defenders guarded the weak spot of the castle and so, where the castle was weak, there it was strong. But the approaches they knew were strong, they left unguarded; and so as it turned out, where the castle was strong, there it was weak.

That is so often the story of human life. Whenever a man falls, it is usually at the point where he thinks he is strong. A man's moral weakness is well-nigh invariably his strong point that goes unguarded. His bad point is his good point that spills over. The worst aspects of a man's life are usually potentially the best in him that gets out of hand. Like Saul, he falls on his own sword. His strength becomes his undoing.

See, for example, how true this is of certain admirable qualities. Take self-confidence—surely an admirable trait. We all admire a man who walks up to a situation with sure step, rather than shaky knees and cold sweat. Yet, how easily can self-confidence become self-conceit, self-assurance arrogance and pride! Out of strength comes weakness.

Or, consider ambition. That, too, is a worthy quality. We think well of the man who likes to get on, to be successful, to

[3] Ernest F. Scott, *The Varieties of New Testament Religion* (New York: Charles Scribner's Sons, 1943), p. 113.

get to the top, and all that sort of thing. Yet, how surely can ambition make a man avaricious and proud, how quickly can it convert a man into a hard-driving go-getter. He has no time for worship, for friendship, for beautiful music or good books, for the little amenities and courtesies of life—no time to live! He gets to the top, but what of it? "What shall it profit a man, if he shall gain the whole world, and lose his own soul?" (Mark 8:36 K.J.V.) Out of strength comes weakness.

Sympathy is an admirable trait. Some people are just naturally friendly, kindly, human, and most of their problems grow out of that fact. Sympathy often degenerates into maudlin sentimentality. Sympathy can convert a man into a sort of Old Faithful, always gushing. Indeed, sympathy may even make one incapable of serving people. For there are times when the best service we may render others is not by speaking soft, sweet words, but strong, even hard words. "Son of man, stand upon your feet, and I will speak with you." (Ezek. 2:1.) Sometimes we do most for others when we act not in the capacity of a nurse who tries to make the patient comfortable, but of a doctor who says, "It is time now for you to get out of bed and go home." The sympathetic often offer indulgence when what is needed is discipline. So, out of strength comes weakness.

If one were to ask, "What value do we cherish most?" would we not say, "Our freedom"? We love freedom more than money. Twice in our lifetime have the freedom-loving nations of the world poured out unstintingly their treasure—wellnigh bankrupting their economy—to defend it. We love freedom more than life itself. Millions have died that liberty might live. Most of us would rather die like men than live like slaves. Here is our strong point.

Consider, then, this treasured possession. We may think of its political aspect—freedom to vote or worship, freedom of press or speech. We may think of it spiritually, as we contemplate the freedom of the will—the capacity with which

God has endowed us as we choose between right and wrong, good and evil, truth and falsehood. But however we think of freedom, is there any doubt that some of the most shocking evils of our day come from the abuse of this very value we so highly cherish? There is an old saying that the best thing becomes the worst thing when the thing goes bad. And liberty, the best thing, easily degenerates into license—the worst thing. Indeed, I wonder if John Burroughs was not right when he said, "The vice and crimes and follies and excesses of society are the riot and overflow of the virtues. The pride of the rich, the tyranny of power, the lust of gain, the riot of sensuality, are all a little too much of a good thing." [4] Out of strength comes weakness.

Of course this truth applies not only to individuals, but to our world. Just where lies the danger to man today? Does it lie in his weakness? No, it lies in his strength. Does his danger come from his ignorance? No, it comes from his knowledge. Does our peril spring from the fact that we do not know how to wage bacteriological warfare, to build rocket planes, or make hydrogen bombs? No, but from the fact that we do know. At the risk of oversimplification, might we say that the evils that started World Wars I and II did not come from a Germany that was weak but from a Germany that was strong. Japan and Italy started aggressive wars and were destroyed not because they were weak but because they were strong. If there should be a World War III—which God forbid—whence will it come? More than likely, out of misunderstandings and unresolved tensions between Russia and the United States. Is it just a coincidence that these two nations are regarded as the two strongest nations in the world today? Ah, Paul, you are right: "When I am weak, then I am strong." And history proves the reverse is true: "Where I am strong, there I am

[4] *Accepting the Universe* (Boston and New York: Houghton Mifflin Co., 1920), p. 78.

weak." As Harry Emerson Fosdick has said, "The idea that we are made great by our superiorities and ruined by our inferiorities is a dangerous half-truth." [5]

It follows in the third place, that in the fact that out of our strength comes our weakness, lies man's undying need of God. For here man faces his dilemma, the paradox of his earthly life. It is a mysterious and tragic paradox that in many instances man never is so insufficient as when he thinks he is sufficient, never so weak as when he thinks he is strong. The evils of his personal life grow out of those very qualities that are potentially admirable. It may not be too much to say with John Burroughs that in some fashion, his vices grow out of his virtues. The very power by which he seeks to make himself secure becomes the main cause of his insecurity. The very knowledge on which he depended, as he said with H. G. Wells that civilization was a race between education and catastrophe —this very knowledge, unless illumined and directed by the wisdom from above, is potentially able to destroy him and all his works.

Whence comes this paradox? What does this mean? The answer in theological language is that man is ensnared and imperilled by his sin. Paul voiced this truth when he wrote: "I see in my members another law at war with the law of my mind and making me captive to the law of sin. . . . Wretched man that I am! Who will deliver me from this body of death?" (Rom. 7:23-24.) From this inner perversion, inner contradiction, which makes my strength, my privileged position, privileged race, my power, the source of so much injustice and evil to my fellows and so ultimately to myself, who will deliver me? One thing is certain: man cannot deliver himself from this dilemma. He is, as it were, mired in the morass of his own inner inconsistencies and contradictions, and his struggle to extricate himself by himself sends him deeper into the mire.

[5] *On Being a Real Person* (New York: Harper & Bros., 1943) , p. 66.

It is impossible, for example, as John Baillie once pointed out, for a proud man, by his own efforts, to overcome his pride, since he would be proud of having done so, and would thus fall victim to the worst pride of all—spiritual pride. There is even such a thing as being proud of your humility, as is evidenced in an autobiographical work published in 1930 in which occurs this sentence: "I have never lost the childlike humility which characterizes all truly great men." [6]

Christianity—a prop for the weak? A crutch for the crippled? Perchance, behind this criticism lies a deep truth. Maybe it is! For if truth be told, we are all weak. We are all finite, sinful mortals "standing in the need of prayer," and none so weak as those who think they are strong. Those who know they are weak and seek the divine aid, in their weakness are made strong. But those who know it not and are deluded by pride and self-sufficiency, are exposed *and expose mankind* to the gravest dangers.

Is not this the problem of our time? I am not one of those who believe that all the evils of our age lie behind the Iron Curtain. Yet, does not the peril of Communism lie in this, that the Communists (by which we mean the rulers of Communist countries) profess to be self-sufficient? They have no need of God. They adhere to no principle—"right is that which serves us." Their pledged word cannot be trusted because they feel no obligation to any truth that transcends them. They are self-sufficient, a law unto themselves. They act as though they were landlords, and forget that they are tenants. In short, the dictator thinks he is God. By some strange quirk whenever mortal man thinks he is God, invariably he acts like the devil. For human strength unillumined by the divine wisdom, unguarded by the divine power, undirected

[6] Quoted in John Baillie, *Invitation to Pilgrimage* (New York: Charles Scribner's Sons, 1942), p. 58.

by the divine spirit, unredeemed by God's grace—such strength today is man's greatest liability.

Unregenerate power is still man's major peril. It was so in the first century, and it has been thus ever since. It was unregenerate power that crucified Christ, the Truth; and that same unredeemed power has been responsible for most of the crosses ever since, whether those crosses stand in the costly and cruel camaraderie of some Flanders' Field, or in the solitary splendor of Calvary.

The gospel has an answer to this tragic paradox of man's life, which makes his strength his undoing. Christianity takes power, robs it of its perverted desire to dominate or destroy, and makes it an avenue of service. It is "the power of God for salvation." (Rom. 1:16.) Is not this the meaning of the Incarnation? For the truth of the Incarnation is that the Omnipotent has revealed himself in Christ—Christ who humbled himself, took the form of a servant, became obedient unto death, even death on a cross, and through the Cross has made power redemptive. This is the profoundest truth of the gospel. It is a truth which our age neglects at the risk of destroying itself. God has revealed in Christ the divine use of power —power used constructively in the service of mankind. From the human use of power as an agent of man's pride, lust or greed, or his sin, we have nothing to hope.

We face here the timeless truth of the gospel—"to you is born this day in the city of David a Savior, who is Christ the Lord" (Luke 2:11). It seems strange to apply the words Savior and Lord to the same individual. They seem the antithesis of each other. A Savior is a servant; a Lord, a master. A Savior offers service; a Lord demands it. But therein lies the mystery of the Incarnation—the Lordship of Saviorhood, the greatness of humility: God born in a stable!

The Cross, then, which reveals this paradox, is the key to the redemption of power. Its message was never more needed, its truth never more relevant than now. For at the Cross the love of power yields to the power of love. At the Cross the humble are exalted, and the haughty are brought low. Here the weak are given strength; and the strong, realizing the perils of power and privilege, are redeemed from the pride that goes before destruction and the haughty spirit that precedes a fall.

IX

God or "Gods"

"Seek first his kingdom and his righteousness, and all these things shall be yours as well."
—MATT. 6:33

WHEN SOMEONE SAYS HE CAN GET ALONG WITHOUT GOD, that does not mean that he gets along without a "god." In a certain sense there are no atheists. When anyone says he does not believe in God, he means, consciously or not, that he does not believe in the God in whom you or I may believe. But, believe in some sort of "god" he does, because he must. A man's God is that in whom or what, he thinks he finds the ultimate meaning of life. Paul spoke of those "whose God is their belly" (Phil. 3:19 K.J.V.) ; that is to say, those who think that life's deepest satisfactions or rewards come from indulging their physical appetites. "Let us eat and drink, for tomorrow we die." (Isa. 22:13.) Life's meaning lies in its ultimate meaninglessness. But to believe in nothing is still to believe.

It is true then that life presents us with a choice—God or "gods." As someone has put it, "Destroy a man's faith in God and he will worship humanity, destroy his faith in humanity and he will worship science, destroy his faith in science and he will worship himself, destroy his faith in himself and he will worship Samuel Butler"; or, one may add, someone far less worthy—Joseph Stalin, for example. Consider then the claims of the Christian's God. Said the Master: "But seek first his kingdom and his righteousness, and all these things shall be yours as well."

93

These words may be taken to represent, broadly speaking, the two aspects of reality—the spiritual and the material, "God" and "things." At the outset, it should be made clear that the choice with which Jesus presents us is not one of alternatives, but of priorities. The choice is not "God" *or* "things," but rather which should come first. There is nothing inherently evil in "things" as such. If there were Jesus would not have said they would be added. An old college professor once said that the mark of an educated man is that he knows how to make an outline. He can distinguish between big "A" and little "a." He knows what to put first.

In the Book of Job, Sheol is described as "the land of darkness . . . without any order." (Job 10:21, 22. K.J.V.) Hell is a disorderly place. If it is, then we can understand why there is so much hell on earth today. Does our trouble lie in the fact that we do not know how to make an outline, what to put first? May we be putting our "gods" before God? An idol need not be a "metal image," it can be a "mental image." Said Martin Luther, "Trust and faith of the heart alone make both God and idol. . . . Whatever then thy heart clings to and relies upon, that is properly thy God." [1]

Let us see some of the things which our hearts cling to or rely upon—the "gods" that we put before God. There are many of them, no doubt. Perhaps the ones we shall mention might not be your choice.

Surely one of our firsts is money. Men still worship the Golden Calf. The Almighty Dollar, though not nearly as almighty as it once was, has for too many of us, taken the place of Almighty God. Now let us make it clear that we are in no sense criticizing the perfectly proper, indeed inescapable, necessity of making money to provide for our legitimate needs and, as far as possible, the unforeseen contingencies of life. What we have in mind is the attitude which makes money

[1] Bernhard W. Anderson, *Rediscovering the Bible*, p. 5.

an end in itself. Sometimes to acquire it, we sacrifice our honesty, integrity, and even our very souls.

It is significant that the first temptation our Lord faced in the wilderness was that of converting stones into bread. It is as though the tempter said to him, "The surest way to win a following is first of all to satisfy man's hunger for material possessions." The fact that he refused does not mean that he deemed the material unimportant. Far from that! Could it be that he wanted first of all to make men aware of God? Did he want to teach them that important as are material things, the deepest truth about man is not an economic, but a spiritual one? The only man Jesus ever called a fool was a rich man. Why was he a fool? Was he a fool because he prospered, pulled down his barns and built greater ones? No! He was a fool because, as his barns grew bigger, he himself grew smaller. He became quite devoid of social concern. "What shall *I* do?" "*My* barns"; "*my* soul"; "*my* goods." Moreover, he seems to have starved his soul to death. "Soul, you have ample goods laid up for many years; take your ease." (Luke 12:19.) He was a fool because he thought he could feed his soul as he did his cattle, from the contents of his barn. He made money his god. He did not own his money—his money owned him.

But money will not do! It cannot be made a substitute for God. Just see what making a god out of money, putting that first, is doing to our country. Fosdick put it well when he said:

College men selling their own games for bribes; . . . one government agency after another disgraced by the greedy peddling of influence; vast syndicates of crooks making millions out of the gambling cupidity of the people; local governments debauched by criminal alliances, corrupting even the officers of the law; men and women making fortunes selling dope to children.[2]

It is a frightening picture!

[2] Used by permission of Harry Emerson Fosdick.

But putting material values ahead of spiritual values, making money our god, not only weakens or destroys our moral foundations, but, strangely enough, destroys the very material things themselves. Many of us, thinking of our retirement, may have bought some insurance policies and put them away in the strongbox of a bank. A thief in broad daylight has entered the bank and, without benefit of key, opened our strongbox, and literally walked off with half of what we had there. The values we put in the bank are worth just one half of what they were. The name of the thief—inflation! We do not want to oversimplify this matter. But is it not true that selfishness and greed lie behind this? We have an insatiable desire for more and more and more. We must "get while the getting is good." We insist on round after round of higher wages, followed by round after round of higher prices, or vice versa, regardless of what happens to the economy. Is there any doubt that this is one of the major causes of inflation, which impoverishes us all? So, strangely enough, when we put money first, the very money itself vanishes in thin air. The way to our material security and well-being does not lie in the philosophy of materialism.

Let us give an example of what it means to put God before money. Every once in a while something happens to uplift our spirits. Such an event occurred a few years ago. A preparatory school in Mississippi, Jefferson Military College, was in dire financial straits and about to close its doors. An interested donor offered the school $50,000,000. That would have put it on easy street. But there was a string attached. In accepting the gift, the school had to promise that it would teach white supremacy; in other words, that it would spend its life propagating a lie. The trustees refused the gift. They realized that there was something more important than money—truth. They refused to put money before God. They knew how to make an outline.

Money, therefore, will not work as a substitute for God. From the days of Judas until now, whenever we betray truth for money, we betray ourselves.

Another of modern man's priorities is power. It has been said that man has three great lusts: the lust of knowledge, the lust of sensation, and the lust of power. Some thinkers, however, have felt that the first two urges are derivatives of the last. Thomas Hobbes the philosopher writes in his *Leviathan:* "So that in the first place, I put for a general inclination of all mankind, a perpetual and restless desire of Power after power, that ceaseth only in death." So we have sought power and we have found it.

Now the arresting fact is that this incredible power which we now hold in our hands, instead of solving our problems, has posed one of our biggest problems. Instead of inspiring confidence, it is making us jittery. It has not given us the sense of security, but has increased our feeling of insecurity. In revealing our strength, it has disclosed our weakness. Instead of making us invincible, it has made us more vulnerable than we have ever been.

There is an Old Testament story which aptly describes the limitations of power. When the armies of Sennacherib, King of Assyria, were encamped around the gates of Jerusalem, a diplomat was sent to Hezekiah, King of Judah, urging him to surrender. One of the inducements made by Sennacherib was this, "I will give you two thousand horses, if you are able on your part to set riders upon them." (II Kings 18:23.) As a matter of fact, this seeming inducement was in reality a taunt. Sennacherib was actually saying this: "You poor Israelites! What chance could you have against me? You are so weak you cannot even provide riders, let alone horses. I would give you two thousand horses if you had riders to put upon them."

His words reveal not only the weakness of the Israelites of

old, but they aptly describe our condition. The great problem of our age is that we have horses aplenty but no riders. Rider-less horses—what a picture of our age! Power without high purpose, power without wise direction, power without ade-quate controls. We have been naïvely acting as though the way to solve the problem of power was just by getting more power. And how we have increased our power! Poor Sen-nacherib's horses are no match for our mechanized steeds, which never tire. Some of them travel faster than the speed of sound, and they "pack a wallop" which makes the Assyrian horses seem like little toy ponies. But this has not solved the problem of power; it has only increased it.

For the real question of power is—power for what? It has been said that the bomb is here to stay, and that the real ques-tion is whether we are. There is truth in the quip that "the way to hell is paved with good inventions." Sir John Ander-son, British Cabinet Minister and director of atomic research and development, has said, "We've opened a door—maybe a treasure-house, maybe only the realization of a maniac's dream of destruction." [3] Will President Eisenhower's idea of con-verting atomic power to socially useful ends come true? The answer to that question, power is powerless to give. The an-swer lies not in power, not in the horse, but in the rider.

A boy was once asked, "What is the most dangerous part of an automobile?" Promptly and wisely he replied, "The driver!" Fortunately our scientists are at long last catching up with that boy. Time was when they felt their duty done if they opened the door to their Assyrian stables and turned a new mechanized steed loose and riderless upon the world. Recently, however, they turned out one of such fearful mien that they are frightened. They now realize that the answer lies not in power, but in the moralization of power. And

[3] Quoted in Gerald Kennedy, *A Reader's Notebook* (New York: Harper & Bros., 1953) , p. 15.

power cannot be moralized until man is Christianized. This is his hope of redemption.

Some words of Plato are apt! "Whenever anyone gives something too big to something too small to carry it, too big sails to too small a ship, too big meals to too small a body, too big powers to too small a soul, the result is bound to be a complete upset." [4] The more thoughtful among us are coming to see that our problem is "too big powers to too small a soul." One hopes it is not wishful thinking to say further that, however dimly, we are beginning to realize at last that in the solution of this problem, it is no use to look to Assyria for our salvation. In Judah, not Assyria, lies the answer to the problem of power. For Judah has always put the emphasis on personality, and on the rider, not the horse. "And you, O Bethlehem, in the land of Judah, are by no means least among the rulers of Judah; for from you shall come a ruler who will govern my people Israel." (Matt. 2:6.)

Christ has revealed a new kind of power, symbolized by a cross: the power of love, the power of goodness, the power of truth; in short, the power of God. This power in the face of all the brutal and boisterous forces in our world, may seem as frail as the reed shaken by the wind. Ah! but it is not! The Cross, symbol of this power, "towers o'er the wrecks of time." It is only as we allow ourselves to be mastered by this power, that we can gain mastery over the frightening and fiendish forces which if turned loose may spell our doom. One can only hope it is not too late.

Let us mention another idol with which we are trying to replace God—liberty. One hesitates to mention this, for liberty is so obviously a priceless possession. It is so close to God. Yet, even this democracy we cherish cannot be made a substitute for God—for in truth it is largely rooted in God. It did not just grow like Topsy, nor did the stork bring it. The

[4] Quoted in *Religion in Life* (Winter, 1953-54) XXIII, 1, 23.

foundation of democracy rests upon our faith in the inherent worth of each individual, regardless of his race or station. Walt Whitman, far-visioned poet of American democracy, said, "The whole theory of the universe is directed unerringly to one single individual—namely, to you." But where did Whitman get this idea? Whence comes this faith in the supreme value of each individual? It is rooted in our Judeo-Christian tradition. One of the sages of Israel, in rich imaginative style, wrote: "When a man goes forth on his way, a troop of angels precede him and proclaim: 'Make way for the image of God, blessed be He.'" His insight found its consummation in the gospel of Jesus, who made the astonishing claim that one human soul was of more value than the whole world.

The situation, then, is this. There can be no reason for believing in democracy unless one believes in the inherent worth of each individual. And there is no reason for believing that, unless one sees on the individual the mark of the Eternal God. But for his relationship to God man has no ultimate value whatsoever. Democracy then has spiritual rootage. As Rabbi Silver has said: "Modern democracy was born out of the struggle for religious freedom in the sixteenth and seventeenth centuries." It is no coincidence that the Liberty Bell has a biblical verse inscribed on it: "Proclaim liberty throughout all the land unto all the inhabitants thereof" (Lev. xxv 10). Samuel Smith, author of "America," wrote:

> Our fathers' God, to Thee,
> Author of liberty,
> To Thee we sing.

Many modern lovers of democracy, however, tend to forget the part which faith in God has played in giving us our liberties. Our modern attitude is best represented by our ten-cent piece, "the smallest silver coin in circulation." On one side of the coin the word "liberty" is spelled out in big letters. In the left hand corner, so small that one almost needs a magnifying glass to see it, are the words, "In God we trust." Does this mean that in our thinking, liberty is more important than God? If so, liberty will lose its meaning. "My child," said Voltaire, "God and liberty. Recollect those words."

> Long may our land be bright
> With freedom's holy light.

But without God freedom's light is never holy. It is cheap and bizarre. For liberty without God is freedom to do what we like when we like, regardless; this is anarchy, slavery. Liberty without God is privilege without responsibility; indulgence without discipline; speed without direction. Liberty without God is the Prodigal saying, "Give me the share of property that falls to me" (Luke 15:12), and then going off to forge his chains. Liberty without God is "the bondage of self-centeredness." It is the liberty of a ship which has lost both rudder and compass. It is frustration. There is little doubt, then, that even this costly and treasured gift, when uprooted from its sacred soil and cheapened by the techniques of secularism, can and does become a means to demoralization and decay, rather than to nobility and enrichment of life.

We have mentioned three of our modern rivals of God: wealth, power, and liberty. But in a real sense, we are wrong. None of these things is evil in or of itself. Each may be the source of blessing. As a matter of fact, God has only one rival —man. It is the stubborn, unregenerate human heart that perverts these things which are potentially good, into actual evil. Out of the heart proceeds all evil, as Jesus said.

Let us close with the testimonies of two great men. The late Archbishop of Canterbury, William Temple, said, "There is nothing, literally nothing—I think there is scarcely a thoughtful man who denies it—that can save civilization, but the incoming of the rule of the unseen and eternal Kingdom of God." [5] And here is a word from H. G. Wells. Unlike the archbishop, he would not be regarded as a particularly religious person—not at least in the Christian sense. Yet from his study and observation of human life, he wrote: "Until a man has found God and been found by God, he begins at no beginning, he works to no end. He may have his friendships, his partial loyalties, his scraps of honour. But all these fall into place and life falls into place only with God." [6]

Truly, God is the supreme reality without whom no other value reveals its real worth. How wise was Jesus, how true his words: "Seek *first* his kingdom and his righteousness, and all these things shall be yours as well." It is as though he said, "Learn how to make an outline."

[5] Quoted in John Seldon Whale, *What Is a Living Church* (New York: Harper & Bros., 1937), p. 37.

[6] *Mr. Brittling Sees It Through* (New York: The Macmillan Co., 1916), p. 442.

X

On Being a Solitary Christian

". . . not neglecting to meet together, . . ."—HEB. 10:25

THE ACHIEVING OF TRUE SELFHOOD, OF WHICH WE HAVE been speaking, has not only a Godward, but a manward side. The Christian religion is rooted in man's knowledge of God and fellowship with him. Fellowship with God in the Christian sense, however, can never be separated from fellowship with "the brethren." "In fellowship religion hath its founts," said George Meredith. This leads us to speak of the Christian church, "the body of Christ," Paul called it. Can the individual be himself in the Christian sense apart from the Christian fellowship? Too many of us Protestants seem to think so. In this we are mistaken.

It is a disturbing fact that in the average Protestant church on any given Sunday, only one third of the membership is at worship. This does not mean that the other two-thirds never attend. In the course of the year they may drop in on occasion. They will probably be present at Christmas, certainly at Easter. But, it does mean that they do not see the importance of worship. There is no regularity in their attendance. It is a hit-and-miss affair, and more often miss than hit.

From New Testament times, getting together for fellowship and worship has been considered an essential part of the Christian life. So the unknown author of the Epistle to the Hebrews writes: "Let us consider how to stir up one another to love and good works, not neglecting to meet together, as is the habit of some, but encouraging one another, and all the more as you see the Day drawing near." (Heb. 10:24-25.) "Not neglecting to meet together, as is the habit of some." Yet, despite this admonition, there are many who feel that they can be good Christians all by themselves, apart from the Christian fellowship.

Consider, for one thing, how surprising it is that Americans, of all people, should form this habit of "neglecting to meet together." Are there any more socially-minded, club-minded people in all the world than we Americans? We are the world's greatest joiners. Yet, the strange fact is that some of these very people who are so punctual and regular in their attendance at their social clubs, luncheon clubs, fraternities, and the like, habitually give the church the absent treatment.

This widespread neglect of worship on the part of two-thirds of the Protestant church members is a serious matter: John Ruskin asked:

> What greater calamity can fall upon a nation than the loss of worship! Then all things go to decay. . . . Literature becomes frivolous. Science is cold. The eye of youth is not lighted by hope of other worlds, and age is without honour. Society lives for trifles, and when men die we do not mention them.[1]

The inconsistency of the solitary Christian, however, is not the most serious aspect of his neglect of worship. Let us see what is wrong with this idea of trying to be a Christian all by oneself, apart from the Christian fellowship.

Well, for one thing the solitary Christian betrays his own nature. Man is by nature a social being. This is why "solitary confinement" is so severe a punishment. If you should sever the relationships that bind a man to his fellows in his home, his business, his civic or social life, he would not be a man at

[1] Quoted in *The Speaker's Bible* (Aberdeen, Scotland: The Speaker's Bible, 1927) p. 192.

all, but a "speculative abstraction." He would be like a tree uprooted from the soil upon which it depends for support and nourishment. The tree would wither and die, and so would the individual. This is true even of the so-called "rugged individualist." The most rugged individualist without his fellows would, to change the figure, be like a boat lying high and dry when the tide recedes. Still a rugged boat, no doubt, but helpless. Separation from one's fellows is not a source of strength, but of weakness.

An individual all by himself has been likened to a word. Now a single word is an important unit. But, it is only as a word is combined with other words, that sentences are formed which convey thoughts, and paragraphs which elucidate meanings. It is true in every area of our life that the key to the enrichment and enlargement of the individual self is found in sentences and paragraphs—not isolated words.

Take one of endless examples. Here is a man who wants an education. Does he say, "Now I will be a solitary student. I will not go to school or college. I will not associate with those who have similar interests or aims"? Hardly. For a large part of his education is in the exchange of ideas, in association with those of like aims and interests. This truth applies to all of life. The language we use, the food we eat, the ideals we cherish—none of these would be possible without the background of society. No man is a man all by himself. As Rufus Jones says, "One person alone is simply nobody at all." [2] And we venture that by the same token, one Christian alone, isolated, separated from the Christian fellowship, is simply no Christian at all.

It is sometimes said that religion is a personal matter—the relationship between the individual and God. And so indeed it is. But there is a vast difference between a religion that is personal and one that is private. A private religion becomes a

[2] Quoted in Harry Emerson Fosdick, *Rufus Jones Speaks to Our Time* (New York: The Macmillan Co., 1951), p. 216.

self-centered religion; and it is precisely from the sin of self-centeredness that Christianity offers us salvation.

Emil Brunner, the noted Swiss theologian, has likened the individual soul to a well-guarded castle: "The possessor of this castle is called 'I.' And everything is operated according to the will of this 'I,' and the laws are *my* laws. . . . Things must go as *I* want them to, and as they suit *me*."[3] Now, it is from that castle of self-centeredness that this unknown writer sought to save us when he wrote, "not neglecting to meet together." Christian fellowship is one answer to self-centeredness.

On a church in Wareham, England there is a plaque which reads as follows:

> Pause ere thou enter, Traveler, and bethink thee
> How holy, yet how homelike is this place
> Time that thou spendest humbly here shall link thee
> With men unknown who once were of thy race.

We need to be linked up. An individual link lying loose all by itself is not itself. If a single word needs other words to give it meaning, so a single link finds its strength and effectiveness as part of a chain. There are too many loose links lying around in Protestantism. "The eye cannot say to the hand, 'I have no need of you,' nor again the head to the feet, 'I have no need of you.' " (I Cor. 12:21.) As an old Quaker, Robert Barclay once said:

> For, when I came into the silent assemblies of God's people, I felt a secret power among them, which touched my heart; and as I gave way unto it, I found the evil weakening in me and the good raised up; and so I became thus knit and united unto them . . . And, indeed, this is the surest way to become a Christian.[4]

[3] *Our Faith,* tr. John W. Rilling (New York: Charles Scribner's Sons, 1949), p. 98.

[4] Quoted by Samuel M. Shoemaker, *The Church Alive* (New York: E. P. Dutton & Co., Inc., 1950), p. 101.

It is as though he were saying, "Don't be an isolated word, a detached link."

But, now let us mention another fallacy in the position of the solitary Christian. Not only does he betray his own nature, he also betrays the nature of the faith he professes. Scholars are now telling us that the roots of the Christian church can be traced to the "faithful remnant" of which the Old Testament prophets spoke. When the Hebrew nation turned away from God to idolatry, the prophets fixed their faith on a remnant. This remnant was a fellowship, a group of people who persevered in God's worship and service. This was the true Israel within the Israelite nation. We are assured that the Christian church today is spiritually continuous with the "faithful remnant." Christianity is thus rooted in the religious community of the Old Testament. From those roots has sprung a tree, the only adequate name for which is fellowship.

Consider the Master. One of the earliest acts of his public ministry was the calling of his disciples. Why? "He appointed twelve to be with him." (Mark 3:14.) These men were at times a handicap to him. They did not always understand him. At times they quarreled among themselves. One of them denied him, and one betrayed him. Yet despite all this, they were invaluable. The truth is that Jesus without his disciples simply could not have been the Jesus we know. Nor did he call these men just to win a number of separate followers, but rather to bind them together in a fellowship. He referred to them as the "brethren."

Indeed the very nature of the gospel he preached would have been meaningless without "the brethren," the fellowship. Surely, it is true that love, service, and the brotherhood of men in God are among the regnant ideas of our Lord. But each of those ideas requires a community in which to be practiced. One cannot love and serve in isolation.

Moreover, as Ernest F. Scott reminds us, before he left them, Jesus held a supper with his disciples, "consecrating them as a community which would cherish his memory and would be reunited with him in the kingdom of God." [5] He said to them: "Where two or three are gathered in my name, there am I in the midst of them." (Matt. 18:20.) This does not mean, as we have been reminded, that our Lord is more likely to be present in a small gathering than in a large one. It means that he is more likely to be present in a community, a fellowship, however small—even two or three—than to the individual who is separated from his fellows. There can be no doubt, then, that the nature of our faith, as exemplified by Jesus, was conceived and expressed as a fellowship.

What was true of him was equally true of his greatest apostle, Paul. Paul was a rugged individualist, if ever there was one. His religion was deeply personal. "It is no longer I who live, but Christ who lives in me." (Gal. 2:20.) Ah, but while his religion was thus deeply personal, it was never private. The first thing he did after his conversion was to have himself baptized as a member of the Church, and wherever he went, his chief purpose was to found churches. "For this reason I bow my knees before the Father, from whom every family in heaven and earth is named, . . . that you, being rooted and grounded in love, may have power to comprehend with all the saints." (Eph. 3:14, 17.) "With all the saints"—in fellowship, community. "A Christian who stood all by himself was unthinkable to Paul." [6]

Indeed, this whole matter of the Christian faith grew out of a fellowship and would have been impossible without it. As we recall the familiar names associated with the writings of the New Testament—Matthew, Mark, Luke, John, Peter, Paul—we might think that the books written by or ascribed to these men came from them as individuals. Nothing could be further from the truth. The Gospels and epistles are the

[5] *The Nature of the Early Church* (New York: Charles Scribner's Sons, 1941), p. 64.
[6] *Ibid.*, p. 148.

faith, not of isolated individuals, but of the Church, the fellowship, the community of believers. The Christian faith we share grew out of the Christian fellowship, "the beloved community," and would have been impossible without it.

In view then not only of the nature of man, but also of the nature of the gospel we profess, how inadequate seems the position of those of us who say that we can be Christians all by ourselves, in isolation from the Christian fellowship. We are not ourselves when we "stand in our own corner alone and fiddle or beat our little drum." Emil Brunner puts it stronger. He writes: "Only in the congregation, only in confessing 'I need the other man' shall you receive God's salvation. Otherwise you remain self-contained—and unsaved." [7]

Finally, let us say that the solitary Christian betrays not only his nature and the nature of the faith he professes, but that, because of this, he makes relatively ineffective his witness for Christ. We are living in a world today that seems to have fallen apart at the seams. It lacks unity. This presents a real opportunity to Fascism and Communism. For these are totalitarian movements. They promise to bind up this fragmentary world into a total whole.

It is a vain promise. Actually, these totalitarian movements have only succeeded in increasing the antagonisms and tensions of our age, making the split deeper and wider. They do this, not only because their methods of intimidation and coercion are divisive, but chiefly because the ideas for which they stand—nationalism, racialism, or economic determinism—are not ideas that can be universalized. The result is that the cure offered by totalitarianism at this crisis of human history is worse than the disease. In their attempt to create fellowship, they destroy it.

Now we believe that Christianity does have a message for this divided world. We believe that fellowship in Christ is a

[7] *Loc. Cit.*, p.13.

truly universal fellowship, because it is "more than merely human." This fellowship into which we are called is more than an association of people. It is an association of people who are held together by that which transcends each and all of them, transcends their differences of race, class, and nation. It is a fellowship in which there is neither Greek nor Jew, barbarian, Scythian, bond or free, but all are one. This is the fellowship our world needs today more than anything else. The solitary Christians weaken this witness immeasurably.

At the beginning of World War II a German student wrote a letter to a British friend with whom he had worked in the Ecumenical Movement. Here is a part of that letter:

> With these lines I have to say farewell to you. We have to expect to be called for military service in Germany. What this means for men like ourselves, who were blessed in these years of friendship and trust, by fellowship and love of Christians all over the world, that cannot now be expressed in words. . . . And now we have to go the way into the darkness. We are not alone on this way. Jesus Christ is being with us. And if the day comes when the light of God and His mercy will shine again upon our peoples and Churches, then do remember, my dear friend, if I am still alive, that there is a friend of yours in whose heart all the spiritual heritage of thirteen years, does not fade away, and who will be ready for all the work of God after this time of great temptation.[8]

The spirit of this German student, finding with his British friend a fellowship which transcends their divergent races, cultures, nations, ideologies, a fellowship in Christ, is the best hope of our divided world. Is it not the only hope? Our solitary Christians weaken this fellowship just at the time it needs to be strengthened.

[8] John C. Bennett, *Christian Idealism* (New York: Charles Scribner's Sons, 1941), p. 148. Used by permission of the publisher, and of the Christian News-Letter, London.

What we have said about the solitary Christian could be said with equal truth about the solitary churches. If the Christian cause is greatly weakened by individual Christians, separated from the churches, it is weakened just as much perhaps by the individual churches separated from the Church. Paul referred to the Church as "the body of Christ," and the obvious mark of the body is its unity in diversity.

At the meeting of the Second Assembly of the World Council of Churches, held at Evanston, Illinois in the summer of 1954, one of the delegates from Africa, Peter Kwei Dagadu, said this:

Any one who has seen four different denominational church buildings standing in a row in a small village, or noted the rapid increase in the number of sects in West Africa, . . . must bear in his heart something of the cost of the disunity of Western Christianity. Africa is paying a high price for it.

Not only Africa, but the whole Christian movement is paying, and doing so in two ways. One is in the evil effects of the sectarian spirit on the individual Christian. Paul recognized this long ago. He rebuked those who were saying, "I belong to Paul," or "I belong to Apollos," or "I belong to Christ." They were to that extent unchristian. The sectarian mind is not the Christian mind. It gives primary loyalty to a partial truth. It diverts the mind from the weightier matters, and makes one more concerned about the growth of his denomination than the progress of the Kingdom. It fosters pride rather than humility, and makes one arrogant rather than teachable. It often lacks the spirit of love. In short, a good sectarian makes a poor Christian.

The other evil lies in the harm done to the Christian enterprise as a whole. United we are strong; divided, weakened and our energies dissipated. The story has it that on a farm near New Haven a farmer's little daughter wandered off and was lost. The neighbors all rallied around, each seeking the child, but in vain. The child's father called them together and said to them, "It is easy for us to miss many places or go to one place many times. Let us join hands . . . we'll then be somewhat like a large rake; then we'll be sure not to skip any place."

This they did. In less than half an hour they found the little girl. She was dead. The anguished father said, "In God's name why did we not join hands before!"

God grant that all Christians will join hands; indeed, that all men of good will who believe in God and reverence truth, will join hands before it is too late.

XI

To What Church Do You Belong?

". . . the church of the living God, the pillar and bulwark of the truth." —I TIM. 3:15

IN SPEAKING OF THE CHURCH, SYMBOL OF CHRISTIAN FEL-
lowship, I am thinking of the Protestant church, the one
I know best. What is said, however, would not, I think, be
inapplicable to Roman Catholicism.

It is difficult to generalize about the church, for the church
is not one, but many. It is made up of millions of individuals
from all walks of life, with the greatest diversity in points of
view, interests, and backgrounds. In its fellowship are the
very rich and the very poor, the learned and the illiterate,
the prominent and the obscure. Whenever anyone says, "The
church is this," we might reply, "So it is. But the church is
also that."

This is what many critics of the church usually fail to see.
Their criticism is often justified as far as it goes, but one
always feels like asking, "What church are you talking about?"
For there are at least three churches, and it is of these that
we speak. Of course, in doing so we shall be running into the
danger of which we have just spoken, namely, generalizing.
Allowance must be made for this.

In speaking of the three churches of Christendom, we are
not thinking of the church in terms of denominations. We
are not asking whether we be Methodists, Episcopalians,
Presbyterians, Disciples, Lutherans, Baptists, or what not.
Such divisions may be thought of in perpendicular fashion.

113

He accepts the comfort and consolation of Christianity, but avoids its challenge and discipline. He tends to regard religion as just another custom or convention, an outward form lacking inner power.

Today people, even people in the churches themselves, think of religion, not as that which is relevant to, and informs, all activities, but as just one activity among others for those who happen to be inclined that way, like folk-dancing. It is something apart. The whole business of religion begins and ends in a situation of abstraction from the things that actually fill men's lives.[1]

There is a wonder story from the Arctic which says that once the flames of the candles froze and the explorers broke them off and wore them for watch charms. The flames congealed and were worn as ornaments. So "the burning words of Scripture, the blazing affirmations of old creeds, on fire at first with the passion of souls possessed by God"[2] become for the conventional Christian congealed, lacking in saving light or warmth.

Such, in brief, is the conventional church.

Now when people criticize the church, it is usually these two churches of which they are thinking. If there were no other church, one fears the picture they draw would be a fairly accurate one. But there is a third church, and this is the one that gives hope as we face the future. Not the reactionary or the conventional, but the "creative" church—the church of the Living God. Members of this church are usually found in every local fellowship, and surely in every denomination.

The creative church is the church that responds to the

[1] Herbert H. Farmer, *The Servant of the Word* (New York: Charles Scribner's Sons, 1942), p. 196.

[2] Harry Emerson Fosdick, *The Meaning of Faith* (New York: Association Press, 1951), p. 278.

leading of the Holy Spirit. It is spiritually awake and alive. Let us see if we can describe it more specifically.

The creative Christians are the courageous Christians. They are courageous, not because they have unbounded faith in themselves, but because they have unbounded faith in God. They are not afraid of new truth—provided, mind you, that it *is* truth. They believe that God is the source of all truth. When some new theory is advanced in the field of science, psychology, or something else, which seems to contradict or change some traditional religious belief, they are not unduly alarmed. They argue that if this new idea is really true, it must be God's truth—for God is the source of all truth, and cannot be divided against himself. Therefore, the creative Christian says with Gamaliel, whose advice in this matter it is often wise to follow: "Keep away from these men and let them alone; for if this plan or this undertaking is of men, it will fail; but if it is of God, you will not be able to overthrow them" (Acts 5:38, 39).

And so, when Copernicus or Galileo or Darwin or somebody else advances some new theory of the universe or human life, the creative Christian does not, first of all, begin to fight them; rather, he begins to listen to them, to try to understand them. He then looks at his traditional beliefs. He tries to distinguish between the essential and the incidental, the picture and the frame, the scaffolding and the building, the treasure and the earthen vessel. He remembers that the men who wrote the Bible or the creeds simply did not possess the knowledge of this mysterious universe which we now have. He therefore enlarges his conception of God and often finds that his faith, far from being destroyed, is purified and enriched.

> He saw the boundless scheme dilate,
> In star and blossom, sky and clod;

117

And as the universe grew great,
He dreamed for it a greater God.[3]

Again, the creative church is the critical church, critical of itself and of society. And, by critical we do not mean the suggestions we sometimes make to each other, which if made and received in the right spirit, can be quite helpful. We mean rather, that this church views itself and its world under the light of the eternal, the ideals of the kingdom of God as Jesus revealed them.

This church does not uncritically accept the standards of society or weakly adopt its practices. The creative Christian asks such questions as these: "What is the true measure of success? Are our material standards Christian? Is the most successful man necessarily he who amasses the largest fortune?"

How is one to regard the liquor business, this modern octopus that is slowly but surely increasing its strangle hold on our corporate life? As one thinks of what liquor is doing to individuals, to families, of the death and destruction it causes on our streets and highways through drunken drivers, of how closely it is allied with all kinds of crime, vice, and corruption, what should be one's attitude as a Christian? Because "everybody's doing it," is that good and sufficient reason why one should?

How is one to regard the ill-advised, if not vulgar, display of wealth in which Americans sometimes indulge? In a world like ours, with its starving millions, is that to be admired or regretted?

What is more desirable for a man, "social standing" or "spiritual power"?

These are some of the questions the creative Christian asks.

[3] Sam Walter Foss, "Two Gods" from *Songs of the Average Man.* Used by permission of the publishers, Lothrop, Lee & Shepard Co., Inc.

There is a disturbing word in one of Paul's epistles: "Do not be conformed to this world but be transformed by the renewal of your mind, that you may prove what is the will of God, what is good and acceptable and perfect." (Rom. 12:2.) To be conformed to the world is not an adequate principle for a Christian. It belongs to the subhuman world. Organisms in the lower orders of life survive by adapting themselves to their surroundings, but not so man. To him is given the power to control and to create his environment. Biologically has this not been the key to his painful climb from animalism? It is, none the less, the path to his spiritual development. Our Lord could say, "I have overcome the world" (John 16:33). That was no easy victory. Too often one fears we are overcome by the world. One thing, however, is certain: whatever victories we win will not be along the path of easy conformity which requires no moral resistance. The creative Christian, therefore, will not blindly or meekly adjust himself to the standards of a secular society. He will rather judge society in the light of that which transcends it, and so will he judge himself. He will not be just an echo of the world's voice, but will seek to be the voice of God to the world.

The creative church is also the pioneering church. It bears somewhat the same relationship to the conventional church that the airplane does to an aircraft carrier. It takes off and explores the possibilities of more effective action. It is the creative church that is striving for Christian unity, seeking some more inclusive and richer fellowship than our fragmentary Protestantism allows, trying to answer the prayer of Jesus: "that they may all be one." (John 17:21.) It was the creative church that worked, and is still working and praying for a just and durable peace. It is this church which is now beginning seriously to inquire whether a church that erects racial barriers to its fellowship is really Christian, whether it is in line with the spirit of him who has broken down the

119

middle wall of partition. This is the church that is concerned about applying the principles of Jesus to the varied problems of our social life.

To be sure, it has no panaceas, no neat ready-made answers to society's problems. But it believes that human problems, unlike scientific ones, need something more than technical knowledge and skill. Human problems are essentially spiritual. Their solution requires a clean heart and a right spirit. In this realm Christ has no peer. This is why the creative Christian believes that Christ is the true light for our dark and dangerous days. In a word, the creative Christian is not content simply to do something *for* the church, he wants to do something *with* it, to make the church an instrument in the hands of God for the bringing of his kingdom.

It is, I think, fair to say that few of us belong completely or all the time to any one of these churches. At times we are reactionary; at times we drift along in our easygoing, conventional manner; and we have moments, when under the leading of the Holy Spirit, we rise to creative heights. But by and large, however, each of us for the most part belongs to one of these churches. For these are the three really important churches of Christendom, stretching horizontally across all denominations—the reactionary, the conventional, the creative.

We cannot close without asking, "To which of these churches would Jesus belong?" One wishes that every religious question could be answered as easily and confidently as this one. Surely we would not find him among the reactionaries. It was the reactionaries who opposed him most bitterly and played so large a role in his crucifixion. "For the sake of your tradition, you have made void the word of God" (Matt. 15:6), he said to the reactionaries of his day. How he chided the reactionaries for their failure to distinguish between the essentials and nonessentials of religion, their tithing mint, anise and cummin and forgetting the weightier matters! He criticized them for their failure to distinguish between the gold, and the altar that sanctified the gold, their keeping the letter of the law and denying the spirit of it. "You have heard that it was said to the men of old, . . . But I say to you. . . ." (Matt. 5:21, 22.)

Nor would he be found in the conventional church, among the easygoing people for whom religion is an outward form, lacking in inner power. He would not be found with the people whose religion makes them conform to the standards of society rather than, like leaven, transform it. Indeed, in the Book of Revelation the Spirit says to the conventional, lukewarm church that is neither cold nor hot, "I will spew you out of my mouth." (Rev. 3:16.)

No! There is no doubt that Christ would be found in the creative church. On the way to Emmaus, when he made as though he would go further, he was finally recognized and the disciples said to him: "Stay with us, for it is toward evening and the day is now far spent." (Luke 24:29.) We would all like to keep Christ with us in our cozy cottages. He stays for awhile as he did with the disciples on the Emmaus road. But then he goes on. He is on the march. He is referred to as the Pioneer of Faith—"he is going before you." (Matt. 28:7.)

No physical symbol ever fully describes a spiritual truth. Henry Pitney Van Dusen, writing of these churches, suggestively likens them to a gigantic body with two small and militant wings and a great hulking center.

At the center is the main bulk of the Church in every age, *the conventional Church*—a fairly representative cross section of the contemporary community, somewhat purified and empowered by contact with its Founder and Lord.

On one side of this large central body is "the *wing of re-*

action—nursemaid of superstition and bigotry, enemy of science, sponsor of Crusades and Inquisition."

On the other side . . . is the *wing of creative life*—mother of the arts, sponsor of the philanthropies, father of reforms, begetter of revolutions . . . unwearying purifier of the conventional Church, yet *always* born from the loins of the conventional Church —its child, its outcast, its redeemer.[4]

Another possible symbol might be a ship. The anchors would represent the reactionaries. Anchors are quite necessary, yet a ship that perpetually lies at anchor is hardly true to its nature.

The largest part of the ship—the hull—would symbolize the conventional church. It is not at anchor, yet seems to lack both direction and power. It yields, conforms easily, to the passing pressures of wind and wave. It follows uncritically the tides of opinion and custom.

The creative church might be likened to the sails spreading to catch the winds of God, and moving in the direction of his purpose. It responds to the leading of the Holy Spirit—God at work in the world, present, active, making his power available for carrying out the eternal purpose which he purposed in Christ.

> Breathe on me, Breath of God,
> Fill me with life anew.[5]

The hope of the Christian cause as it faces the future lies in the creative church: a church that is courageous because it trusts God, the source of all truth; critical, because it views itself and its world under the light of the eternal; adventur-

[4] *Life's Meaning* (New York: Association Press, 1951) , p. 96. Used by permission of the publisher.
[5] "Breathe on Me, Breath of God," Edwin Hatch.

ous, because it follows One who is on the march, goes before us—the Pioneer of Faith. To be a member of the creative church is to join the church to which Christ belongs. This is, in the words of the apostle, "the church of the living God, the pillar and bulwark of the truth." (I Tim. 3:15.)

XII

The Task of the Church Today

". . . for such a time as this."—ESTH. 4:14

THE TITLE SUGGESTS THAT THERE MAY BE SOMETHING ABOUT today which differentiates it from yesterday. There is. Let us mention at least two ways in which this difference appears.

For one thing, our age is more closely knit, its life more interwoven than ever before. Under the magic of science, distance has disappeared. It is now measured not in miles, but hours. Our world has become quite small. In such a world, isolationism is dead and buried without the slightest hope of a resurrection. This is by no means an unmixed blessing. For while science has given us proximity, it has not and cannot give us community; and proximity without community spells trouble. Our world testifies to this. It is a world in which our frictions and tensions have been sharpened and intensified. We can no longer live without each other, and have not learned to live with each other. That is the heart of our problem. For unless we learn to live together, it is doubtful if we shall live at all.

There is another factor. Our age is a dynamic one. It is in ferment. The common man the world around is waking up and is never going back to sleep. He is becoming aware of *his* inalienable rights. He is on the march, and in no foreseeable future will he come to a halt. Communism is, unfortunately, the diabolical means through which his long-smoldering resentments are being kindled, his buried hopes liberated. It is little use to tell the underprivileged of the earth that communism is a false hope, a delusion, and a snare. To the hopeless any hope, even a false one, is better than no hope. Drowning men do grab at straws.

A dynamic world is a dangerous world. Hence, our life is imperilled. And yet, the dynamic ages of history have been the creative ages. God can do more when the waters are stirred than when they are stagnant.

Such, then, is this age of ours—closely knit and widely revolutionary. In such an age the Church of the Living God faces its task. What is its task?

Of course, the task of the church in our age is fundamentally no different from what it has always been. The eternal truths of the gospel do not change with the changing years; they are "the same yesterday and today and for ever." (Heb. 13:8.) The task of the church today, therefore, is essentially the same one the first-century church faced; namely, to make known to men the redemptive love of God revealed in Jesus Christ our Lord. While, however, the task remains the same, the peculiar problems or perils of each age throw new light on that task, place it in a new perspective. It is the glory of Christianity, a mark of its vitality, that it is an adaptable religion. It can change its emphasis without altering its nature. Just as a tree changes from year to year, even century to century, and yet remains the same tree, so does Christianity, the tree of life whose leaves are "for the healing of the nations." (Rev. 22:2.) Let us suggest three ways in which this healing may be made available. Here lies, in part at least, the unique contribution of the church to our troubled times.

For one thing, the creative church can help to sensitize the conscience. A Canadian broadcaster has recently stated our case in a single sentence: "An uneasy conscience makes a better Christian than a sense of moral complacency." Ibsen's *Peer Gynt* heard a sermon once, and his comment was: "Well, *that's* what I call Christianity! Nothing in it to make me feel uneasy." Actually, that is what should not be called Christianity. "The infection of an uneasy conscience" has been one of the great contributions of the creative church to human progress. Kagawa calls conscience "the sword point of evolution." I like to think of it as the growing edge of personal and social progress.

Unquestionably the conscience of the world was affected by men, like Francis of Assisi, whose self-dedicated, self-giving lives mediated the concern of Christ. Wesley also, in his mission to the miners to whom he preached in the fields, and William Booth, with his interest in the unwashed of London's East End, have widened the area of Christian concern—as have others like them.

All of us know how conscience operates in our personal lives. Each of us knows that he is "a moral personality under orders." Like Joseph, when confronted with some moral issue, we have said, "How then can I do this great wickedness, and sin against God?" (Gen. 39:9.) But the present age is making it clear that while the task of the church in producing men of personal moral integrity is basic and indispensable, it is not enough.

Indeed, it was not enough in Jesus' day. He spoke once to a rich young ruler whose moral life was impeccable. He had kept all the commandments from his youth. But Jesus made him feel uneasy, sent him away sorrowful. Jesus, figuratively speaking, put a window in the wall of his moral fortress and made him look out upon a world from whose suffering and need he had been insulated. I suppose that no one has done as much to awaken the social conscience and thus to widen the area of our concern as has Jesus of Nazareth. "He stirs up the people," said his enemies.

Consider the experience of John Woolman, the renowned Quaker of the eighteenth century. The plight of the slaves was on his conscience. He wrote:

I saw a mass of matter of a dull gloomy collour, between the

126

South and the East, and was informed that this mass was human beings, in as great misery as they could be, and live, and that I was mixed in with them, and henceforth I might not consider myself as a distinct or Separate being.

In infinite love and goodness he hath opened our understandings from time to (time respecting) our duty toward this people, and it is not a time for delay.[1]

I believe that if God in his mercy could have opened the eyes of the privileged people of the world in general, and of Tzarist Russia in particular, to their duty to the unfortunate, and if they could have realized, as did Woolman, that there was no time for delay, we might have been spared the curse of communism. It is very difficult not to regard communism as the judgment of God upon a civilization that had lost concern, concern for the very people, the underprivileged and dispossessed, whom Jesus in the temple at Nazareth made the primary object of his ministry. These are the people who now see in communism a flame of hope.

The initial step in the correction of any evil is an aroused conscience, and the church can help create that. What institution is better fitted to do this? What other is so well fitted? None!

Another area of the church's task is that of helping to develop a Christian mind or approach to life's problems. "Let this mind be in you, which was also in Christ Jesus." (Phil. 2:5 K.J.V.) Jesus told his disciples that they should be in the world, and yet not of the world. Surely this is not easy. It is like asking a man to go in the water without getting wet! The most Christian among us, involved in the complexities of our secularized civilization, will come up, if not soaked to the skin, at least somewhat damp. Making allowance therefore for the well-nigh inevitable compromises in which we are all

---

[1] Quoted in Willard L. Sperry, *Stranger and Pilgrims* (Boston: Little, Brown & Co., 1939), pp. 155, 159.

willy-nilly involved, it is nevertheless true that there must be a Christian way of looking at life.

Certainly there is a communistic way of looking at it. When all is said and done, the most terrible thing that the dictators have accomplished is not that they have added so many thousands of square miles to their empire. It is rather what they have done and are doing to people's minds. They are indoctrinating men with a new set of "ideals" and ideas. Millions of people are now looking at life in a way they never did before. They have, as we say, a new "ideology." Incidentally, this is why we cannot destroy communism with bombs. Communists may be stopped by bombs, but not communism. For communism is essentially an idea, a faith. It is something in people's minds and hearts. *That* cannot ultimately be killed with bullets.

In the early days of the Christian church, the Roman Empire thought that the way to stamp out Christianity was to kill the Christians. And Christians were slaughtered by the thousands. But that did not stop Christianity; no more will it stop communism. Enough good and evil men have been killed to prove that we cannot stop either goodness or evil by killing people. Ideas have to be fought with ideas. A wrong way of looking at life has to be overcome by a right way of looking at it. How true are Paul's words: "We are not contending against flesh and blood, but against the principalities, against the powers, against the world rulers of this present darkness, against the spiritual hosts of wickedness in the heavenly places. Therefore take . . ." What? A stock pile of bombs? No—"The whole armor of God." (Eph. 6:12, 13.) In the long last it is only truth that can vanquish error. This is why we say that surely a part of the task of the church in the present age is to try to discover, develop, and project in society the Christian way of looking at life.

What is this Christian way? Let me just point out one of its characteristic features.

There is a most illuminating text in the Book of Leviticus. The children of Israel had escaped from Egypt and were about to enter the Promised Land. This is the command that God gave them through Moses: "You must not copy the practices of Egypt, where you lived, nor the practices of Canaan, whither I am taking you; you must not rule your lives by theirs. Follow my regulations, keep my rules, and live by them; I am the Eternal your God." (Lev. 18:3-5 Moffatt.)

I believe that was the beginning of the Christian way of looking at things. It was a way that could not be identified either with the practices of Egypt which they were about to leave, nor yet those of Canaan whither they were going. It was that in the light of which both Egypt and Canaan had to be brought to judgment. The Christian way of looking at life therefore was not the Egyptian way of looking at it, nor the Canaanitish way. It is not necessarily the Democratic way nor the Republican way. It is not necessarily the "Fair Deal" way nor the "Free Enterprise" way. It is not the way of "rugged individualism" nor of uniform collectivism. It is the way by which all our ways are brought to judgment.

Gilbert Baker, in discussing the problem which the Christian church faces under the Chinese-Communist regime, uses a figure which is suggestive. He writes:

The Christian is perhaps like a sea bird following a ship in its plodding way, resting on the ship too. But the bird lives in another dimension, it makes rings around the ship, it can see better than the captain which way the ship is going, and yet it is the captain that has to steer the ship, not the bird. Yet there is something hopeful about the bird, for when he sees it, the captain knows that he is going in the right direction, and it may give him hope.[2]

[2] "The Christian Church Under Non-Christian Rulers," *Theology Today* (April, 1950), p. 93.

It is the task of the church then to bring a "vertical dimension" to bear on our common life and in so doing "to seek to leaven and redeem society in the name of Christ."

The church should try to recapture the spirit of Isaiah's remnant. The remnant was "an Israel within an Israel," a spiritual minority who viewed life under the light of God's truth. Those whose minds are benumbed by partisanship or blinded by prejudice have little to contribute today. Those who are 100 per cent Democratic, 100 per cent Republican, American, Baptist, Methodist, or anything else will make slight contribution to this complex and chaotic age. The truth is that none of us is 100 per cent right or true or good. "All we like sheep have gone astray." (Isa. 53:6.)

There is much talk about producing people who are completely adjusted to their environment. Some of it is salutary and helpful. Many of us face conditions comparable to Paul's thorn in the flesh. We cannot get rid of it. We have to live with it. And many, like Paul, through God's grace have made of their thorn, not a source of irritation, but an avenue through which life has been mysteriously enriched and ennobled. But much of this adjustment philosophy is misleading. If the rear wheels of our car are stuck in the mud or snow, the car may be said to be completely adjusted to its environment. But the trouble is that it is stuck! What is needed is a lever to lift those wheels to a higher frame of reference. It was such a lever that Christ brought to the world. Pilate—there was a perfectly adjusted individual for you! The man who stood before Pilate was not so adjusted, nor can anyone be who shares his spirit. Only that which transcends the world can help the world. It is only the Kingdom which is not of this world that can redeem the kingdoms of this world.

The church has had courageous souls who have not conformed to the world, but have sought to reform it. Luther was such a reformer. His "Address to the German Nobility," published in August, 1520, "was a ringing appeal to the German Emperor, princes, and nobility to take in hand the reformation of Germany, religious, ethical, social, and economic." "Your princes have become the companions of robbers," he tells the nobility, quoting Isaiah. And fittingly did he quote Isaiah, for the prophets were the fearless heralds of God's judgment on a society that spurned his righteous will. We must not allow our faith in God's goodness to obscure his severity, nor in his mercy to minimize his judgment.

Here then are two contributions the church can make to the present age. It can help create a Christian conscience, and so widen the area of social concern; view the current scene under the light of the Eternal, the impartial judgments of God, and so point men to the truth which alone makes men free.

There is a third aspect of the church's task which we barely mention. The church needs to acquire some technique for implementing its ideals. Some boys who were studying Christianity were asked by a businessman if they ever read or studied the Bible. They said they did not. When their teacher was asked why the Bible was ignored, he replied, "We teach religion by atmosphere." The businessman countered, "How long will it take to redeem the world through teaching the principles of Christianity by the atmosphere method?"

Now, atmosphere is very important in the propagation of Christianity. Indeed, it has been said that Christianity is not so much "taught" as "caught." But the atmosphere created by a socialized conscience and a Christian view of life needs some social implementation, some technique, to make it effective. Is this, in part at least, the meaning of Jesus' words, "The sons of this world are wiser in their own generation than the sons of light"? (Luke 16:8.)

Some years ago Harry Emerson Fosdick preached a sermon on the subject "Making Goodness Attractive." A sermon needs to be preached on "Making Goodness Effective." For example, in a recent year America spent $101 on each of its white pupils in tax-supported schools, and $12 on each negro pupil. The state of Mississippi in the same year spent $45 on each of its white boys and girls, and $5 on each of its negro children. Now, not all the good will or sense of fair play in our hearts can of itself change that situation. Our Christian consciences may be aroused by such conditions, and we may bring a Christian mind to bear on them; but that alone will not be enough to altar such situations. Only legislation can change them—some technique through which our good will can be made effective.

There are grounds for hope. For example, it is hard to overestimate the work of the National Council of the Churches for a just and durable peace. Moreover, should we not be encouraged by the vast difference in spirit and purpose between, let us say, the Versailles Treaty of World War I and the Peace Treaty with Japan of World War II? However imperfect that treaty might be, surely it records an honest attempt to give social implementation to the Christian ideals of justice, forgiveness, and good will. We need and must have more of that sort of thing. Whatever may be the shortcomings of the so-called "social gospel," there is no doubt that men like Washington Gladden, Walter Rauschenbusch, and others, sought to give social implementation to Christian ideals.

The late Wallace Petty used to say, "What the church needs is not more saints but seers." In other words, not more goodness, but more wisdom in making goodness effective. Jesus said, "Be wise as serpents and innocent as doves." (Matt. 10:16.) It is not enough in this age to be as innocent as doves. We need more of the wisdom of the serpent.

Here, then, are some of the areas of the church's task. How is this task to be accomplished, and by whom? The answer lies with the laymen. The Protestant layman, however, will need first of all to discard two entirely un-Protestant ideas before he is able to perform this task. One is that religion is primarily, if not exclusively, the business of clergymen, as though the layman's place were that of a spectator in the bleachers, rather than a player on the field. This was one heresy that Luther attacked. "Every believer is a priest," he said. That is to say, every layman shares *equally* with the clergy the privileges of the gospel, and consequently has as much responsibility for spreading it as any ordained minister, priest, bishop, or even the Pope himself.

The second un-Protestant attitude to be discarded is that which regards the church as an institution standing at the corner of Fourth and Main, rather than an organism. The Protestant layman must realize that in a real sense he does not go to church, but that *he* is the church. The church is a living organism. "You are the body of Christ," said Paul (I Cor. 12:27); not the bricks, stone, or mortar. This was another of the heresies Luther attacked. He said the true church was invisible; its strength could not be measured by material standards. Too many laymen, as Elton Trueblood has reminded us, think of church work as that which goes on within four walls, as though God's business were confined to weekends. The truth is that the great issues and decisions of our day are not made in church buildings on Sunday morning, but every day of the week in the workaday world, where the business of life goes on. More Protestant laymen must take the strength and inspiration of Sunday morning into homes, factories, offices, into politics, education, industry, and witness *there* by word and example to the reality and truth of the gospel.

To the degree that the average layman realizes that he shares *equally* with his minister the responsibility of spreading the gospel, and that the real church is not a building or institution, but living individuals who bear witness to the gospel by word and life in all areas of life—to that extent will the church be getting on with its redemptive task.

XIII

The Gospel and Society

"Repent, for the kingdom of heaven is at hand."
—MATT. 4:17

WITH THESE WORDS THE MASTER ANNOUNCED HIS PUBLIC ministry. While we do not intend to discuss them in detail, we use them because they reveal the two sides of his message. "Repent." This was his call to personal regeneration. "For the kingdom of heaven is at hand." Thus he voiced the age-long social hope.

Perhaps one of the reasons why the term "social gospel" is held suspect is that Jesus never used it. Indeed, it is not to be found in the New Testament. Consequently it appears at first sight to be something extraneous, a man-made invention, an appendage stuck to the gospel by ill-advised, though well-meaning people, but unrelated in any vital way to the heart of Jesus' message.

Not only so, but the phrase seems impersonal. It leaves us cold. It is vague. Moreover, it challenges us with a task that seems bewildering. It lifts our sights too high. It is hard enough to change the individual, let alone try to make a dent on society, or to think seriously of the redemption of the world.

Then again, the "social gospel" is not "spiritual" enough. It seems materialistic. It appears to concern itself primarily with external changes rather than inner transformation. It lacks the warm devotional qualities which we are accustomed to associate with spirituality. Consequently, to protect the true nature of our faith, we must keep our religion out of business and out of politics. It must not become directly involved in complicated international forums where diplomats wrangle. To relate our religion to the social problems of life makes it commonplace, cheapens it, exposes it to the danger of being secularized. It may become little more than a glorified sort of sociology. It may cease to be leaven and become part of the lump.

However understandable or sincere such opinions may be, they have little or no support in the New Testament. That the gospel from its inception had social implications is seen in the fact that the evils that opposed Jesus, and were ultimately responsible for his death, were all rooted in the society of his day. He was not crucified by those guilty of gross personal sins. He was not crucified by those whom society deemed its enemies. He was crucified by a society who regarded him as its enemy.

Now there are just two types of people we have in mind today. On the one hand, we are thinking of the church people, religious folk—there are such—who are unaware or unconcerned about the social implications of Christianity. On the other hand, we have in mind those who are deeply involved in plans for social betterment but who treat lightly—if they do not quite ignore—the religious faith without which their social idealism has no rootage.

Consider then the first group. They have been known to justify their position by saying something like this: "Jesus had no interest in social problems. The world in which he lived was rife with such problems. There was slavery, tyranny, war, intemperance, and the like, yet he made no head-on attack upon such evils. He was concerned not with problems, but with people. Not even with people en masse, but as individuals." This is quite true. The thing, however, such folk often fail to see is that this very emphasis of the Master on the individual, his inherent dignity and worth as a child of God, inevitably opened the door and blazed the trail to social change.

Evidences of this are not lacking in the New Testament itself. For example, Jesus was not concerned about the breeding and fattening of pigs. Yet once in bringing peace to a disordered personality, a herd of pigs was lost. As a result he was asked to leave the territory. (Matt. 8:34.) His ministry to the individual brought him willy-nilly into an economic problem. Similarly, Paul was not concerned about the industrial problems of his age. Yet when he tried to protect the people of Ephesus from the superstitions of those who feathered their nests by making and marketing silver shrines of the goddess Diana, he became involved knee-deep in an economic problem and barely escaped with his life. The opposition, one suspects, grew not from the avowed fact that their religion was challenged, but that their trade was threatened.

These incidents are important not just in themselves, but because they reveal the motive that undergirds all genuine efforts at social betterment. When we concern ourselves about social problems, it is not because we are interested in the problems as such, as though we were trying to solve a theorem of Euclid, but rather because we see what evil conditions do to the people involved. Is not this, for example, the motive that keeps us trying, despite persistent obstacles, to abolish war? We see now what war does directly or indirectly to people, how it destroys not only our bodies but our souls, since it completely denies everything the Master said about the worth of man, the individual.

This emphasis of Jesus on the individual becomes the key to the "social gospel" from another angle. In his view the individual had not only rights, but duties. Of those who have been given much, much is required. But on those who have been given little, only one talent, the obligation rests none the less. Jesus never regarded the individual as though he were isolated or insulated from society. The salvation he offered to the individual was not salvation from his relationships with other people, but in those relationships. "Repent," he said. To repent is to change one's mind, and to change one's mind is to adopt a new attitude towards God and man. The secret of this new attitude is love. "We know that we have passed out of death into life, because we love the brethren." (I John 3:14.)

Let us consider one or two examples of this. Zacchaeus, a chief publican of Jericho, was a rich man—rich, no doubt, because in collecting taxes for Rome he looked out for number one. Jesus goes to Zacchaeus's house and something happens that changes Zacchaeus. He says to Jesus, "Behold, Lord, . . . if I have defrauded any one of anything, I restore it fourfold." (Luke 19:8.) He begins to consider others. Jesus answers, "Today salvation has come to this house." (Vs. 9.) But this salvation was not something that transpired within Zacchaeus, the individual, and stayed there. Not at all. The proof that he had found salvation was that this inner, personal change reached out into his social relationships. He stopped robbing people. One wonders how many homes in Jericho were affected socially because of his repentance.

Or again. Slavery was one of the great evils of Jesus' day. Neither he nor his leading apostle, Paul, ever attacked it, though they could not have been blind to its tragic effects. Indeed, Paul returned a runaway slave, Onesimus, to his master, Philemon. With the slave, however, he sent a letter to Philemon. It reads in part:

I appeal to you for my child, Onesimus, whose father I have become in my imprisonment. . . . I am sending him back to you, sending my very heart. . . . that you might have him back for ever, no longer as a slave but more than a slave, as a beloved brother. (Vss. 10, 15-16.)

Paul did not attack slavery. No. But he now asks a slave-owner to treat his slave in the spirit of love. How long, one wonders, could Philemon treat Onesimus as "a beloved brother" and still keep him a slave. The truth is that oppression in all its forms not only betrays the inherent worth and dignity of the oppressed but also plays havoc with the principle of brotherly love which keeps man from being an oppressor. The fact that sections of the Christian church stood with the slaveowners shows how many sea miles, religiously speaking, they were from the most elementary, yet revolutionary teaching of Christianity.

Here, then, is one reason why we cannot escape the social implications of the gospel. Though our Master did not attack social evils as such, yet by his emphasis on the value of the individual, and by making of love the guide to our individual acts, he made it impossible for us to avoid them.

But now let us turn to the second group we have in mind. We refer to those social-minded folk who are deeply involved in all worthy programs of social betterment. They serve on civic committees, spend their lives usefully, unselfishly in the service of their communities; but they seem to have little interest in religion in general, or the church in particular. These they seem to consider irrelevant. If pressed about their religious beliefs, they might answer, "My religion is the Golden Rule," or "My religion is the Sermon on the Mount." It is as though they were saying, "My religion is ethics." They are all for the ethical teachings of Jesus, which they seem to regard as the heart of his message.

It is not difficult to understand this position. Indeed, one is sympathetic with this view, for on the face of it so much of Jesus' teaching, so many of his parables, reveal his ethical concern. But this view is untenable. It is impossible to separate the ethical teachings of Jesus from their religious moorings without doing violence to both. As E. F. Scott has pointed out, there is hardly an ethical insight of Jesus that did not grow out of his religious faith.

Consider a few examples of this. He tells us that we are to forgive until seventy times seven. But why should we forgive? Because it is the smart thing to do? No! Because God forgives. He bids us be merciful. Why? Because it is the kind thing to do? No! Because your Heavenly Father is merciful, kind to the unthankful and ungracious. He bids us love our enemies and do good to those who hate us. Why? Because it is a magnanimous gesture? No! Because that is what God does—"He makes his sun rise on the evil and on the good, and sends rain on the just and on the unjust." (Matt. 5:45.) We are to show brotherly concern even for the least or weakest member of society because "their angels always behold the face of my Father who is in heaven" (18:10). He concludes his Sermon on the Mount with what have been called the most daring words ever spoken: "You, therefore, must be perfect, as your heavenly Father is perfect." (5:48.)

These references, to cite no others, make it plain that in Jesus' teaching, religion is the root of which ethics is the fruit. One could not have existed without the other. It was the fact that his religious contemporaries had so largely separated them, that drew his fire and aroused their ire. Wounded men lay on the roadside while the religious people passed by on the other side. That was not their concern. Rich men fared sumptuously while beggars languished at their gates. Prosperous people pulled down their barns, and built greater ones with no sense of responsibility for those whose barns were empty, or who had no barns at all. It is no wonder that a religion so lacking in ethical sensitivity and social concern had become bogged down in trivialties, the tithing of mint, anise, and cummin. It presented an imposing front, lacking inner vitality and power.

But if the separation of religion from its ethical implications is bad for religion, do the ethically concerned see what might happen to their social idealism if, in their ethical zeal, they ignore the religious moorings?

One ventures to say that there is probably more social mindedness, more ethical sensitivity, in our country today than ever. Witness the perennial victory of our Red Feather campaigns. Think of the millions we give annually to our humanitarian and character-forming agencies. But what happens to this ethical concern of ours if it loses the Christian rootage from which it grew? Elton Trueblood thinks we are on the road to losing that rootage now. He speaks in a now familiar phrase of our "cut-flower civilization." That is to say, here are these beautiful flowers, the ethical and moral values, cut from the trees our fathers planted. But those trees were planted by faith, watered and nurtured by prayer and devotion. Now we pass through the garden, cut the flowers, and walk off with them, sever them from their roots. But cut flowers will fade, never mind how many aspirin tablets we put in the water. Should the Christian ethic ever become secularized, might it not lose its meaning?

If we doubt the danger of this, might not communism, an extreme example though it be, give us food for thought? Many will agree that in its inception there was some ethical idealism in communism. Indeed, its pretensions to idealism are even now the source of its strongest appeal to the underprivileged. What has happened to make communism, which started off with some idealism, one of the most brutal, heartless tyrannies in history? Is not the answer the complete severance of its life from all religious orientation? Man is not a child of God, but simply an economic animal whose destiny is fulfilled when his material necessities and wants are met. Since he bears no relationship to that which transcends him, he has no intrinsic worth of his own. His value is a purely utilitarian one. That is what happens to a society which regards religion as a pious irrelevance. Its avowed aim is social betterment, but because its aim is divorced from all religious orientation, the so-called betterment has created more problems, more evils, than it has removed. Under this regime, man becomes a means to an end, not an end in himself. He becomes a tool in the hands of tyrants to carry out their egotistic and tyrannical purposes. Communism's dream is now a nightmare.

From this I believe we may learn a lesson. The key to a better society is not found simply in better houses, bigger cars, more money and the like, necessary and important though such possessions may be. The truth is that materialism is not of itself, can never of itself, be the true measure of man the individual or of his society. If our zeal to improve society begins and ends on this level, we may end up by degrading the very people we seek to uplift. There is a harsh word in the book of Revelation. "For you say, I am rich, I have prospered, and I need nothing; not knowing that you are wretched, pitiable, poor, blind, and naked." (Rev. 3:17.)

This neglect of religion on the part of some ethically minded folk might indicate a deeper error. After all, our social conscience springs from our moral sense, the feeling that we *ought* to do something. But where did we get this sense of moral obligation, this conscience which tells us we ought to consider others, and not just ourselves? Is this something we created, a purely human invention? Is it nothing more than an indication that we are good sports?

We cannot believe this. We cannot believe it, for the feeling of moral obligation causes us at times a great deal of inconvenience, if not real hardship. It does not seem reasonable to suppose that one would knowingly impose on himself something that often makes such heavy demands upon him. The ancient Hebrews with true insight said that the moral law had its source in God, that it was the mark of God, the image of God, in man. Should it ever be generally or widely believed that it has no sanction greater than our inclination, that might well be the end of morals for those who share that

141

view. For if man made the moral law, there is no reason why he cannot amend it or repeal it if he sees fit to do so. But that is precisely what he cannot do! He cannot do it because it is rooted in that which transcends him—in God who created and endowed him with it. Sever it from this rootage, and we shall lose it. Lose it, did we say? No, rather *we* shall be lost! For when we throw the moral law out of the window, we discover that we have only thrown ourselves out.

It would seem evident then that the separation of religion from ethics—the "personal" from the "social" gospel—or of ethics from religion—our social idealism from its religious mooring—is wrong. It damages both religion and ethics. And no wonder, for it mutilates the teachings of Jesus. His first message was, "Repent"—the "personal gospel"; "for the kingdom of heaven is at hand"—the "social gospel." These two emphases were in our Lord's thinking all of a piece. They were not like two halves of an apple. We can cut an apple in two, throw away one half, and eat the other. The part we eat is still apple. The relationship we have been discussing is more like the two sides of our hand. There is no way of separating the palm from the back without destroying the hand. Some tickets are marked, "Not good if detached." That is the relationship between religion and ethics. Detach one from the other, and we damage both; we violate not only their history but their nature.

Religion and ethics belong together. The "personal" and the "social gospel" are one and the same. Without ethical concern, religion becomes a sterile formality, an empty form. Without religion, ethics loses its meaning. If Jesus moralized theology, it is our task to theologize morality. If he humanized the divine, it is our task to, if I may coin a word, "divinize" the human. Our task is to keep together what God has joined together. Only by keeping them together, can religion be saved from sterility and irrelevance, and ethics from secularization if not ultimate destruction.

XIV

When Jesus Entered Politics

"Hosanna to the Son of David! Blessed be he who comes in the name of the Lord!   —MATT. 21:9

To "ENTER POLITICS" HAS A CONNOTATION WHICH DOES NOT apply to Jesus. He did not, of course, enter politics in the generally accepted meaning of these words. Yet the plain truth is that when Jesus was brought before Pilate, he was charged with being a political revolutionary—"He stirs up the people," said his accusers. (Luke 23:5.) He was charged with disloyalty to the emperor. "We found this man perverting our nation, and forbidding us to give tribute to Caesar, and saying that he himself is Christ a king." (Luke 23:2.) "If you release this man, you are not Caesar's friend; . . . We have no king but Caesar." (John 19:12, 15.) He was crucified because ostensibly he was an enemy of the state. The charge of course was false; yet we cannot but see its political implications.

He assumed his political role in a dramatic way. It was the Passover season. Thousands of Jews from the far-flung areas of the Roman Empire had come to Jerusalem to celebrate the Passover. This celebration was not only religious. The Jews of Jesus' day had identified their religious faith with their political aspirations. The Messiah for whom the first-century Jews were looking was just as much a political figure as a religious one. He was to throw off the Roman yoke and restore the kingdom of Israel. It was on this Passover occasion, when the religious-political hopes of his people were running high, that Jesus sent his disciples for a colt, mounted it, and made a dramatic entrance into Jerusalem. The people, no doubt, saw him then as the long-expected political deliverer. He allowed his people to acclaim him king. "Hosanna to the Son of David! Blessed be he who comes in the name of the Lord! Hosanna in the highest!" (Matt. 21:9.)

The fact that ere the week had passed, he who had been the center of attraction became the center of hostility, as acclaim turned to condemnation, may lead us to regard the whole affair as a "flash in the pan." This would be a serious error. If we pass the events of Palm Sunday through a sieve, though many of them slip through, some remain. Let us consider some of the enduring truths suggested by the Palm Sunday episode. This we shall do by asking a few questions.

For one thing, "Why did Jesus assume this role?" At the very outset of his ministry, he had rejected the role of a political Messiah. This was in part the meaning of his temptation, when he refused the kingdoms of the world and their glory. Why, then, did he assume it now?

The key to the answer is given, I believe, in his message to Herod, who wanted to kill him: "Go and tell that fox, . . . 'I must go on my way today and tomorrow and the day following; for it cannot be that a prophet should perish away from Jerusalem.' " (Luke 13:32, 3.) "He set his face to go to Jerusalem." (Luke 9:51.) Why Jerusalem? Because Jerusalem was not only the religious, but the political center of his nation's hopes. Jerusalem was the key to the situation, the crucial point. What happened in Nazareth or Capernaum was important, but what happened in Jerusalem was decisive. I share the view of those who believe that the Master was not content to keep his message just to individuals, but was impelled to bear witness to the nation. He was not content that God's domain be limited to the periphery. God claimed, too, the citadel, the center. Jesus, therefore, wanted to bring the truth of his message into the open, into firsthand contact with the powers. He did not regard the gospel as a hothouse plant living a sheltered life. The gospel rather was to be leaven influencing the whole lump of life. We do not, of course, mean to say that Palm Sunday was the only occasion on which Jesus made clear the social implications of his message. This idea is implicit in his ministry. The salavation he preached meant changed relationships, not only to one's self and to God, but to one's fellow men. On Palm Sunday, however, what was always implicit was expressed in concrete and dramatic fashion.

We need to be reminded of this. We have a witness to bear to the nation. God claims the total life of man. The fact that the church belongs to God does not mean that the state belongs to the devil. Palm Sunday reminds us that the redemptive work of God is for all of life, including Jerusalem. Christianity cannot evade, but must face the problems—economic, social, political—of the day. It was to this truth that Jesus bore witness when he appeared at the head of a throng of pilgrims and received their acclaim. The fact that he was not the sort of king they envisioned, and that the king he really was they did not want, does not invalidate the significance of the event.

Another question comes to mind. "What did he find when he entered Jerusalem?" Speaking broadly, there were three currents flowing into the life of the city. Each stemmed from a different source. There were the people, the Passover pilgrims. They wanted a national hero to restore the kingdom of Israel—they were looking for someone to take a sword and lead a revolt against Rome. On the other hand, there were the Roman officials, Pilate and his official family. They wanted anything but that. Rome gave the Jews considerable liberty in their religion, but one thing Rome would not tolerate—any politically minded Jew who sought to challenge Caesar's authority. Here, then, were the common people who wanted a political Messiah, and the Roman powers to whom a political revolutionary was anathema. In between was a third group, people like the Sadducees. They were collaborationists. They played both ends against the middle. Ostensibly loyal Jews, they yet co-operated with the Romans. They had no desire to revolt against Rome because they received constant favors at her hand. They knew on which side their bread was buttered.

That is what the Master found. And what did he do about all this? Whose side did he take? The people's side, of course, for they had the votes. No, the Romans' side naturally, for they had power. Here was prestige and privilege. No, if he were wise, he would take the in-between side; for then like the Sadducees, he could feather his own nest. I do not believe such thoughts ever occurred to him. Jesus was a strange politician. He took no sides. The key to his attitude is in the song of the Palm Sunday pilgrims: "Blessed be he who comes in the name of the Lord." He took God's side! Jesus went into politics on God's side—"in the name of the Lord." Above all the chaotic and conflicting claims of men he was guided by the claims of truth.

Since he took God's side, he could not stand with the people, give them what they wanted. Under the circumstances what they wanted was impossible. No puppet ruler could break the Roman yoke. Many futile attempts had proved that. The power of Rome, as it happened, was broken by Christ, but not that way.

He could not take God's side and stand with Rome. He had often voiced his opposition to the selfish use of power. "It shall not be so among you; but whoever would be great among you must be your servant." (Matt. 20:26.)

Nor could he take God's side and stand with the Saducean priests, the dishonest men, who were looking out for number one and had converted the Father's house into a den of thieves. He could not identify the cause of righteousness

146

and truth, God's cause, with any of these factions. And so on Palm Sunday he came *not* in the name of the people, *not* in the name of the rulers, *not* in the name of the special-interest group, the Sadducees. He came "in the name of the Lord." When he was being tried before Pilate as a political revolutionary, he said, "For this I was born, and for this I have come into the world, to bear witness to the truth" (John 18:37).

Now let us try to see what bearing the historic situation we have sketched may have on our time. The condition we confront is by comparison so vast, so complicated and involved, that one may deem the Palm Sunday episode wholly irrelevant. We do not think so. There is a timeless truth here. Is it this? Jesus entered Jerusalem "in the name of the Lord." He was guided by the stars, not the street lights. He was loyal to that which transcended the conflicting opinions of his contemporaries, loyal to the claims of truth and righteousness— to God.

Can it be that the key to the redemption of politics lies here? Does it not lie in those big enough to give their loyalty to the truth that transcends policies of expediency and opportunism? A distinguished Peruvian once said, "It would seem that God kept religion for Himself and handed over politics to man." [1] No wonder Lester Ward could write, "In politics, we are still in the Stone Age." [2] We make progress here, as elsewhere, only as we give to God the place that is rightly his, and come to see that in betraying truth, we betray ourselves.

Let us see now what effect the application of this principle, that Jesus revealed long ago, would have on our present-day political life.

[1] Quoted in John A. Mackay, *A Preface to Christian Theology* (New York: The Macmillan Co., 1941), p. 167.

[2] Quoted in Charles A. Ellwood, *Man's Social Destiny* (New York and Nashville: Abingdon Press, 1929), p. 115.

It would mean for one thing that the individual politician would put the best interests of his community above his own selfish interests. The man who enters politics to feather his own nest, look out for number one, betrays the trust of those who have elected him and is unworthy of their confidence. He contributes nothing towards the solution of the problem; he merely aggravates it, makes it worse. We have nothing to hope from this type of individual. How grateful we should be for our honest public servants who are guided by some principle that transcends "the miserable aims that end in self." But for such men, to whom politics is an opportunity to serve the public good rather than an occasion for personal aggrandizement, one wonders what would become of us.

This principle, if applied, would mean something else. Selfishness and greed are not less sordid or harmful if they are centered in a political party rather than an individual politician. If the best interests of his community should transcend those of the individual politician, so should the best interests of the country transcend those of the party. And here again, it is only "in the name of the Lord," of a truth that is above the shortsighted interests of the party, that this can be achieved. It was said of Pericles that he was a good Athenian, but a bad Greek. It can often be said of us that we are good Democrats or Republicans, but bad Americans. We put the success of our political party above the best interests of our country.

This is done in two ways. One is by willfully blocking and defeating legislation that is manifestly right, for no other reason than that it is initiated or sponsored by the party that is wrong—which always is the opposing party. "Her Majesty's loyal opposition" is essential in a democratic society. But when the opposition springs from a base desire to obstruct, to defeat the opposing party for political reasons regardless of the merits involved, then the opposition is not loyal—it is evil. This sort of thing, it seems to me, is shamefully un-patriotic. And it is common practice!

The other way in which the interest of the party is made to transcend that of the country is by using political power to buy votes. By this we mean yielding to the wishes of pressure groups. The more votes the group represents, the more surely we yield. Abraham Lincoln defined democracy as government of, by, and for the people. He meant *all* the people. When either one of our major political parties governs in the interests of *any one* group, it is to that extent no longer government of *the people*.

As far as either of these methods of playing politics goes, there is little or nothing to choose between the Democrats and the Republicans. Putting the "outs" in and the "ins" out, does not solve the problem. There is an old Turkish proverb which says, "The saddles are changed, the donkeys are the same"—or the elephants, as the case may be. We need more than a change of saddles, we need a change of hearts. We need a new awareness of the fact that love of country and devotion to her best interests should transcend our party prejudices and vote-getting manias. None of us wins when the country loses. Here again, we must gratefully acknowledge that in both parties there are truly patriotic men who are Americans before they are Democrats or Republicans and who love their country more than their party. To such men we owe a debt greater than we know.

With what we have said so far, there may be general agreement. There will not be with what we now say. But it inevitably follows. If a great step towards the redemption of politics is that of putting the welfare of the community above the selfish aims of the individual politician, and the welfare of the country above that of the party, it follows that the third step is that of putting the welfare of humanity above the selfish interests of the country.

Some years ago, after its editor had died, the *Denver Post* carried an editorial about him which was intended to be of a laudatory nature. In part it said, "He was first for Denver, second, for Colorado; third, for the Mountain States; fourth, for the United States—and there was *no fifth*." [3] In our modern world, however, there is a fifth, and this fifth stands at the top of the agenda. However reluctant we are to admit it, the truth is that the nations, surely the free nations, are bound together in one bundle. We may win or lose in our fight for freedom, but it seems clear that whatever we do, we shall do together. It is no longer possible for any one nation to maintain a little oasis of freedom in a desert of tyranny. No nation today can ride at anchor in a snug, sheltered harbor when a storm lashes the waters of the world. If the free nations are strong, our own position is made more secure. Conversely, we are weakened by whatever impairs their security. It is in our best interests to promote their best interests. And this we sometimes fail to do.

Consider our Reciprocal Trade Agreement Act. There are two ways of helping the free nations: by direct aid and by trade. The free nations cannot buy from us unless they sell to us. Yet we erect tariff walls so high as to well-nigh close the door to their goods. Any attempt to lower these walls arouses strong opposition. Some local industry—textiles, farm products, oil, watches—may be hard hit. Perhaps so. Yet in view of the world situation, is it not better to bring even temporary hardship to some locality by lowering tariffs than, by keeping them high, endanger the economic well-being of the free nations on whose strength our own national security depends? Economic nationalism does not seem to work with political internationalism. Enlightened self-interest is not the highest motive, yet often our well-intentioned actions are neither enlightened, nor do they promote the best interests of our country. In this modern age our best interests are insep-

[3] Quoted by Samuel McCrea Cavert in Sam Nader, *Sermons for the New Age* (New York: Morehouse-Gorham Co., 1948), p. 112.

arable from the best interests of mankind. J. B. Priestly, in his *Faraway,* makes a character say:

> It's not a matter of Englishmen and Frenchmen . . . it's a matter of men and women. . . . Every time you ignore national boundaries you bring the possibility of a sane, happy, peaceful world a bit nearer. I'm an Englishman and I love England . . . I owe a lot to England. But I owe still more to the world. You say . . . let's do something for England for once. But I say, for God's sake let's do something for civilization for once.

This, it would seem, was the lesson Jesus was trying to teach us when he entered the confused and complex life of Jerusalem. He envisioned above all its nationalistic ambitions the kingdom of God, the *universal* reign of righteousness and truth. The coming of that Kingdom is our daily prayer. Surely we help answer that prayer as our little loyalties give way to larger and more inclusive ones; when, like our Master, we come not in our name, the name of our party, or even of our country, but of a truth which transcends all these, and by which all life is redeemed. We are redeemed by truth, not trickery.

Let us ask a final question: "What happened to the man who came 'in the name of the Lord'—in the name of truth?" He was killed. In trying to please God, he displeased everybody. He displeased the people because he would not give them what they wanted. He displeased the Romans because they thought he was giving them what they did not want. He displeased the Sadducean priests because he dared to attack their shameful trading in the Temple. He therefore aroused bitter opposition. This is usually society's reaction to the true prophet.

Three men were crucified on Calvary's hill long ago—two because they were too bad, and one because he was too good; two because they fell below the accepted standards of society, and one because he rose above them. The surest way at times to "get in wrong" is to stand for what is right. But it is those who do so stand that are the saviors of mankind.

Society is still wont to crucify its saviors! One who enters politics intent on putting the cause of truth above partisanship, courts political suicide. Perhaps this is why there are not more honest and able men in politics. But what a disgraceful reflection this is on you and me, the public. We blame our politicians. Should we not, rather, blame ourselves? Their political fate is in our hands. Too often we have refused to support honorable men, or return them to office, because they stand for principles that conflict with our selfish aims or petty prejudices. We get no better than we deserve.

Palm Sunday shows us that it is not easy to be both popular and prophetic. Said the people of Hosea's time: "The prophet is a fool." (Hos. 9:7.) In truth, however, he is "the watchman of . . . God, yet a fowler's snare is on all his ways, and hatred in the house of his God." (vs. 8.) But the true prophet has the unique assurance of knowing that in speaking for God, he is blazing the path, the only path, to man's redemption. This is seen in the fact that though we kill the prophets, yet we garnish their tombs. We crucify them, yet look wistfully to their cross in its untarnished splendor, believing that somehow in it lies ultimately our salvation.

This belief, history confirms. Every upward step on the path to man's true progress has been marked by the footprints of those who were willing to sacrifice themselves for an ideal. These are the sons of the dawn, the heralds of the new day.

XV

Prices and Values

"To what purpose is this waste?"—MATT. 26:8

WHEN JESUS ENTERED JERUSALEM IN THE NAME OF THE
Lord, he was crucified. He was crucified because he envisioned and espoused a scale of values not shared by his
contemporaries. He viewed life one way; they, another.

Whenever the gospel is taken seriously, it leads to a reap-
praisal of values, personal and social. The late Archbishop of
Canterbury, William Temple, once said that this life of ours
is like a vast store window in which pranksters have switched
the price tags so that things of greatest value are priced as
worthless trinkets, while cheap trash is made to appear as
most valuable. This observation comes from the fact that
William Temple had experienced in Christianity a new scale
of values.

We shall not attempt to discuss values in general, but shall
view them in the light of a familiar New Testament story.
Once, when Jesus was dining in Bethany at Simon's house, a
woman poured a cruse of "exceedingly precious ointment"
on his head. The disciples were "indignant." "To what purpose is this waste?" they asked, "for this ointment might
have been sold for much, and given to the poor." Of course
they were right, it could have been. But is it not too bad to
be so practically shrewd as to be esthetically stupid? Jesus
did not share their view!

Why do you trouble the woman? For she has done a beautiful thing to me. . . . In pouring this ointment on my body she has done it to prepare me for burial. Truly, I say to you, wherever this gospel is preached in the whole world, what this woman has done will be told in memory of her. (Matt. 26:10, 12-13.)

The disciples were price conscious, but not value conscious. The box of ointment to them meant so much money and nothing more. It seemed a shame to waste it. If sold, the money obtained could have served a useful purpose. It might have been given to the poor or it could have been invested profitably. But, as it happened, the ointment was just thrown away. Even the recipient of this gracious act was no better off in any practical sense. There was nothing to show for it. However, in their overemphasis on the utilitarian aspects of this act, they missed the imponderables. What were some of the values that escaped their notice?

For one thing they failed to see the beauty of this woman's act. "She has done a beautiful thing to me," said Jesus. In a sense beauty is useless—a beautiful sunset, for example. One cannot eat it, wear it, buy it, or sell it. But the value of beauty is immeasurable. Indeed, scientists are now telling us that one turning point in man's life came some twelve thousand years ago when man began to adorn his caverns and caves, and put beautiful decorations on his tools and weapons. The caverns would not shelter him more securely because they were adorned, nor the weapons be more deadly because they were decorated. The importance of the emergence of the esthetic sense was not in what was happening to man's weapons but to himself—his soul, his real self, was coming to birth. He was beginning to realize that "life is more than food." (Luke 12:23.) Lecomte du Noüy says:

These *useless* manifestations— . . . mark the most important date in all the history of mankind. . . . The primitive "useless" ges-

154

tures of man are in reality the only ones that count. They carry the germ of abstract ideas, of spiritual ideas; the germ of the idea of God . . . The germ of morals, of philosophy, and of science.[1]

Some years ago a Chinese delegate to one of our American summer conferences delighted his audience as he tried to point out the different reactions of an Indian, a Chinese, and an American upon seeing Niagara Falls the first time. He said the Indian would become deeply meditative, his mystic soul stirred to commune with the Infinite Spirit. The Chinese, with his ingrained sense of family solidarity and loyalty, would wish that his family might enjoy it with him. The American, however, would react quite differently. Upon seeing the Falls, he would immediately begin figuring out how much horsepower was going to waste per minute! No doubt this observation is more clever than true, but there is truth in it. I am rather inclined to believe the story of the American child who, upon seeing a rainbow for the first time, exclaimed: "Oh, Mummy—what is it advertising?" Well, it is advertising something that needs very much to be advertised in our highly industrial and commercial age, in which we seem to see almost everything through the dollar sign. It is advertising the intrinsic values of life, things like beauty which have value for their own sake—not only for what they do for us, but for what they mean to us. Said Charles Kingsley, "Never miss an opportunity of seeing anything beautiful. Beauty is God's handwriting." Indeed it is! And it is written everywhere, from a dewdrop to Niagara, from the smallest flower that grows to the starry heavens. How Jesus fed his soul on it! He saw God's handwriting not only in the lilies of the field, the sunsets, or the face of a child, but in the grass which today is and tomorrow is cast into the oven.

[1] *Human Destiny* (New York: Longmans, Green & Co., 1947), pp. 125, 126.

If thou of fortune be bereft
And in thy store there be but left
Two loaves—sell one, and with the dole
Buy hyacinths to feed thy soul.[2]

But once more, the disciples in their preoccupation with the price of the ointment, missed not only the beauty, but the meaning of this gesture. Here was a woman for whom Jesus had done much. He had redeemed her life from sin, restored her self-respect, opened up the possibilities for victorious living, and helped her find her true self. The disciples could not see in this gesture such values as gratitude, love, adoration, humility, faith. The box of ointment meant to them so much money which could be converted into practical use, but the meaning of this woman's deed was lost.

Is not this, in a nutshell, one of the basic troubles of our time? With our industrial ability, supplemented by our scientific "know how," we have built a material civilization that is amazing. But I wonder, do we ask—to what end, for what purpose, what does it all mean?

The meaning of life is not found by improving our means, but by clarifying our objectives. How we have improved our means through our amazing techniques! The telephone and the radio have increased the range of our voices and the sensitivity of our ears. The microscope and telescope have enlarged our eyes. The automobile has incredibly increased the strength and speed of our legs, the airplane has equipped us with wings more powerful than any bird. The hydrogen bomb has given to our arms a strength of which all the giants of fiction and history never dreamed. But to what end, for what purpose? Thoreau predicted that our scientific inventions would be improved means to unimproved ends. Unfortunately, his prediction has been too largely fulfilled.

When Stanley Baldwin was prime minister of Great

[2] James Terry White, "Not by Bread Alone," *Current History*, August, 1907. Used by permission.

Britain, one of his political opponents said of him that if he started a debate on the "soil of England," he invariably ended it by speaking of the "soul of England." Good for Mr. Baldwin! For are we not now seeing what happens to the soil, the material aspects of reality, when the soul, the immaterial in which alone the ultimate meaning of life is found, is neglected or underdeveloped? Someone has said, "If you lose your sky, you will soon lose your earth." A considerable amount of our earth has been lost. Billions have gone up in the fire and destruction of two world wars, and the end may not be yet. Is this because we have lost our sky? We measure success too largely by material standards only. We tend to evaluate the worth of a man by what he has, not by what he is. But materialism simply does not have the answer to life's meaning. Carlyle's caustic phrase points up the danger we confront: "Soul extinct, body well alive."

Is not this one weakness of secularized education? In many instances education is not concerned with meanings, but with practical, utilitarian considerations. Charles William Eliot, for forty years distinguished president of Harvard, defined education as "the enthusiastic study of subjects for the love of them and without any ulterior motive." [3] We have gone a long way from that. Our motto seems to be, "The shorter the learning, the sooner the earning."

Not only does the utilitarian emphasis obscure cultural values, but in some instances there seems to be a positive aversion among certain educators to spiritual values. The president of one educational institution put this bluntly: "I would discharge any teacher whom I knew to be guilty of bringing moral and spiritual values in the classroom. We're a state teacher-training institution." [4] One cannot believe

[3] Quoted in Walter Moberly, *The Crisis in the University* (London: SCM Press, Ltd., 1949), p. 37.
[4] Kenneth I. Brown, *Not Minds Alone* (New York: Harper & Bros., 1954), p. 177.

157

that this represents the opinion of mature educators. As a matter of fact, an education that omits spiritual values is as effective in saving mankind, as reading a lecture on gravity or the chemical composition of the water in which he is being engulfed would be in saving a drowning man. An education which makes us price conscious but not value conscious, that teaches us how to make a living but not how to live a life, that gives information without direction, facts without interpretation, will not help us. "Improved means to unimproved ends."

It is here that the ministry of Jesus speaks to our condition. He came to help us discover life's meaning. In the world to which he came, the real was the visible. Even the religion of his people had become materialized. It had largely degenerated into the mechanical performance of outward acts devoid of inner meaning. Pharisaism in large measure had lost its soul. Jesus was not opposed to the material aspects of reality. He was no ascetic. He prayed, "Give us this day our daily bread." He healed sick bodies and fed hungry people. Indeed, Christianity has been called, and rightly so, the most materialistic of the world's religions. But Jesus never regarded materialism as an answer to life's deepest meaning. Once, as he observed worshipers casting their gifts into the treasury, he said that the smallest gift made that day, the two mites of a widow, was actually the largest because of the motive of sacrificial love that prompted it. This gave the gift a meaning not found in those given out of abundance. Jesus always looked beyond outward act to inner meaning, to values.

Peter once said to him, "Lo, we have left everything and followed you. What then shall we have?" (Matt. 19:27.) It was as though he were asking, "What do we get for being Christians?" Luke, I believe, gives the answer which comes nearest to Jesus' spirit: "Your reward will be great, and you will be sons of the Most High" (Luke 6:35). You will get something, Peter, but primarily you will *be* somebody. The reward for being Christian is not primarily in getting, but in being. "The fruit of the Spirit is love, joy, peace, patience, kindness, goodness, faithfulness." (Gal. 5:22.) Such qualities have meaning in themselves. They are their own reward.

The utilitarian does not quite understand this. Benjamin Franklin said that honesty is useful because it assures credit. That may be true, but it is not Christian. The greatest reward for being honest comes from the inner satisfaction of knowing that one is trying to be an honest man. If that assures credit, well and good. If it does *not* assure credit, well and good. Christianity is its own reward. It asks no other. How beautifully does the late Willard L. Sperry voice this truth:

There is little or no doubt that the mind of Christ finds a more congenial environment in the studio where beauty is loved for its own sake and not because it pays, on the ship's bridge in a gale where duty is loved for its own sake and not because it pays, in the science laboratory where truth is loved for its own sake and not because it pays, than in the average modern church where the preacher is busy with the sorry argument *ad hominem* in behalf of a Christianity commended to moral investors because it offers large material returns on the spiritual venture.[5]

Finally, let us say that the disciples failed to see not only the beauty of this act or the meaning of it, but also its enduring quality. "Wherever this gospel is preached in the whole world, what this woman has done will be told in memory of her." (Matt. 26:13.) There is in all our hearts the hunger for permanence, for something that will last. We long to feel that through the changing texture of life there is an unbroken and unbreakable thread that gives continuity and lasting significance to our experiences. We long to set our feet upon some solid rock beneath the sinking sand, to put our

[5] Willard L. Sperry, *The Discipline of Liberty* (New Haven: Yale University Press, 1921), p. 130. Used by permission.

hands upon some anchor that holds sure and steadfast amid the gale. Man lives in two worlds, the world of nature and the world of grace, the world of things seen and temporal, the while he hungers for the things not seen and eternal. On the sarcophagus of an Egyptian mummy were found these words: "I am a child of earth and of starry heaven." "Starry heaven"—I am a part of something permanent and enduring.

This desire for the timeless and enduring is seen currently in our hunger for security, which has become almost an obsession. It is natural and understandable that we should want security. But there is no ultimate security for man in materialism—neither in his possessions which either he leaves or which leave him, nor in his body which returns to the dust whence it came. Man's only ultimate security is in God, through whom he discovers the eternal values to which his life may be related. The psalmist's words could be spoken to us. Comparing material with spiritual values he says: "They will perish, but thou dost endure; they will all wear out like a garment. . . . and they pass away; but thou art the same, and thy years have no end. The children of thy servants shall dwell secure." (Ps. 102:26-28.)

The day after the First World War had broken out, August 5, 1914, Sir Edward Grey, who was then Foreign Secretary of the British government, wrote a letter to a musician who had delighted him by his rendition of one of Handel's works. Here are a few sentences from that letter: "I love Handel's music, and it does me good. Europe is in the most terrible trouble it has ever known in civilized times, and no one can say what will be left at the end. But Handel's music will survive." [6] So it has! So it will! For that is the final glory of life's intrinsic values—they endure. Prices fluctuate and depreciate. The dollar is worth half of what it was worth a few

[6] Quoted in Leslie D. Weatherhead, *This Is the Victory* (Nashville: Abingdon Press, 1941), p. 157.

years ago. Intrinsic values do not fluctuate. In God's economy there is no inflation. After commercial and utilitarian values decay, life's intrinsic values abide. The mark of God is upon them, they bear the impress of the Infinite.

How well does the life of the Master illustrate this truth! This gracious gesture of Mary, who poured the ointment on his head, was symbolic, he said, of his own outpoured life. Had you and I been watching the darkening scene on the first Good Friday, might we not have said something like this: "Too bad he had to die—a young man with so much to live for. Why did he not compromise the truth? He was offered the kingdoms of the world and all the glory of them, yet he gave up all this for the eternal values of righteousness and truth. I heard him saying to Pilate, 'For this I was born, and for this I have come into the world, to bear witness to the truth' (John 18:37). He said that was what life meant. Too bad he felt that way. 'To what purpose is this waste?' "

Yet the kingdoms of that world and their glory, which he was offered, have long since turned to dust. And since then others have fallen also—three of them, Italy, Germany and Japan, before our eyes. Who knows how many others might yet turn to dust. But this we know—Christ will survive. He is imperishable. The mark of God is upon him. He is the incarnation of those intrinsic values which neither moth nor rust doth corrupt nor thieves break through and steal. Walter Horton puts it well:

Against us and our kind, wars and revolutions may succeed; but against Christ, to win is always to lose, and to lose is to win. Christ abides in our midst. It is possible to crucify him afresh. But from each fresh crucifixion he must arise again as Victor, for the eternal God is in him.[7]

7 *Our Eternal Contemporary* (New York: Harper & Bros., 1942).

It is our faith that as we live with his spirit and for the values for which he died, we too experience the eternal life he came to bring.

Whatever else be lost among the years
God still abides, and love remains the same,
And bravery will glimmer through men's tears,
And truth will keep its clean and upright name.
As long as life lasts, there will ever be
Kindness and justice and high loyalty.

In a bewildered world these things will hold
The human heart from darkness and despair:
Old as the sun and moon and stars are old,
Remaining constant, they are ever there:
Lode-stars for men to steer their courses by,
The eternal things of life can never die.[8]

[8] "Eternal Values." Taken from: *Light of the Years* by Grace Noll Crowell. Copyright Harper & Bros., 1936. Used by permission.

XVI

Striving for the Unattainable

*"Not as though I had already attained . . . I count
not myself to have apprehended . . . I press toward
the mark for the prize of the high calling of God in
Christ Jesus."* —PHIL. 3:12-14 K.J.V.

THERE ARE SOME OF US NO DOUBT WHO HESITATE TO AC-
cept Christ and the Christian way of life, as we have tried to
present it in this book, because Christianity is too difficult.
Its ideals are too high. Its goals are too remote. It asks too
much of us. We just don't feel up to it. Let us think then
about striving for the Christian ideal.

And, I suppose, the first thing we ought to say is that the
Christian ideal is unattainable. Consider a few of its demands.
"Whatever you wish that men would do to you, do so to
them." (Matt. 7:12.) Do we live up to that? "You shall love
your neighbor as yourself." (Matt. 19:19.) "Love your enemies and pray for those who persecute you." (Matt. 5:44.)
"Whoever would be great among you must be your servant."
(Mark 10:43.) Do we live up to that? "Take . . . no thought
for the morrow." "Your heavenly Father knoweth that ye
have need of all these things." (Matt. 6:34, 32 K.J.V.) "Seek
first his kingdom and his righteousness." (Matt. 6:33.) Do
we live up to that? "You, . . . must be perfect, as your heavenly
Father is perfect." (Matt. 5:48.) To that?

We would all agree that it is not easy to keep the Ten
Commandments. Yet, it is easier by far than to live up to the
Sermon on the Mount. The Rich Young Ruler said he had ob-

served all the commandments from his youth up. But when confronted with the challenge of the gospel, he felt it was too much for him. "He went away sorrowful." (Mark 10:22.)

As a matter of fact, it is too much for all of us. Consider Paul for example. Surely if any man went all out for the gospel, if any man as we say "gave it all he had," it was he. "I count everything as loss," he once said, "because of the surpassing worth of knowing Christ Jesus my Lord." (Phil. 3:8.) Yet did he feel he had measured up? On the contrary, he said: "Not as though I had already attained, . . . Brethren, I count not myself to have apprehended: but this one thing I do, . . . I press toward the mark for the prize of the high calling of God in Christ Jesus." And if Paul said he had not reached the goal, what can you or I say? For this is one of the strange things about Christianity—those who may seem to you and to me to have measured up, would be the last ones to say they had. Paradoxically enough, if they did think they had, that would be proof positive that they had not.

Shall we say then that the Christian ideal is impossible of attainment? That none of us ever measures up to it? That the last word of any of us will be, "I count not myself to have apprehended: . . . I press toward the mark"? Suppose we express the same truth a little differently. Suppose we say that Christianity presents us with an ever-receding goal.

Let us then look further at this unattainable, ever-receding goal with which Christianity confronts us. Quite frankly there are some things to be said against it. It might be said, for example, that having such a goal is likely to produce people who are hypocritical. They think they are living up to it, when in reality they are not. Again, such a goal might produce people who are Christian in name only, nominal Christians. They say to themselves, "If a man like Paul could not reach it, why should I even bother to try? If those who, from my point of view, come so close to it insist that they are still far away, the thing is hopeless." Such people then may bear the Christian label, but make no serious attempt to live the Christian life.

Once more, this unattainable, ever-receding goal might be very hard on conscientious people. They try hard to live up to it, take their religion seriously, as we say. Then, realizing that they come short, they begin to condemn themselves. They are overcome with the sense of their unworthiness. They become discouraged. They develop guilt complexes, or at any rate an unhealthy state of mind which is harmful and unwholesome.

And if it is bad for the individual, since it may produce those who are hypocritical, or nominally Christian, or mentally or emotionally upset, it is equally bad for society. It generates the feeling that Christianity is after all impractical. It just will not work, and so it's no use to take it seriously. A Mohammedan once said to a Christian whom I happen to know, "You Christians preach monogamy, but you don't practice it. We don't preach it. We accept polygamy as being inevitable. You preach peace, but you are always fighting. We know that war is inevitable, so we accept force as an unavoidable necessity."

These are some of the arguments used against the Christian ideal, this ever-receding goal which we seem unable to reach. And that there is some truth in them cannot, I think, be denied.

But now let us point out some things on the other side which we are wont to overlook.

For one thing, we ought to see clearly that difficult, unattainable though the goal with which Christianity challenges us be, that goal is inevitable. Anything less would contradict or betray the very nature of Christianity. For Christianity claims to be the revelation of God. The truths it presents are not the result of man's discovery merely, but of God's revelation. Christ came to reveal God. That was the purpose of his coming. Since this was so, his primary concern, as John

Knox reminds us, was not to tell us something that we might deem practical, but to tell us what was true. His purpose was not to reveal what we are able to accomplish, but what God asks of us. Anything less than absolute truth, never mind how difficult, even impossible of attainment, could not be a genuine revelation of the Holy God, who as the hymn says is, "perfect in power, in love, and purity."

Let us take a simple illustration. Suppose, for instance, that there was some great artist, a painter or musician, with whose work we were unfamiliar. We are anxious to have a sample of his work and request it. The painter says to himself, "These people really cannot appreciate great art. It is beyond them. I shall just hurriedly dash off some little picture and send it to them." In like manner the musician says, "All they can appreciate is jazz. Why should I bother to interpret for them the work of one of the masters? I shall give them what is within the present reach of their appreciation." In such an event, we should get something cut down to our size, but we should not get the real nature of the artist. His creative powers, his talents, his artistry, would remain hidden from us.

It is even so here. Anything less than what Jesus has given us, beyond us though it surely is, would not be a true revelation of God.

God's requirements are absolute and have no reference whatever to the ability of men to fulfill them. Jesus who said, "Be ye perfect as your heavenly Father is perfect," also said, "Why callest thou me good? There is none good but one, even God." [1]

"Not as though I had already attained, . . . I press toward the mark." And I think the Lord would have said to his devoted apostle, "That's all right, Paul. Don't be discouraged.

[1] John Knox, *The Man Christ Jesus* (Chicago and New York: Willett, Clark & Co., 1941), p. 43.

My purpose was not to give you something you could attain, but to show you what the absolute goals are, and have you strive for them."

This leads us to say something else. These receding goals for which we strive, yet never fully attain, are the key to man's progress. They are not meant to discourage us, to be an obstacle to us. They should, on the contrary, be an incentive to effort. At least that is how we regard them in other areas of our experience. Actually, what progress could we have made in any field, but for these ever-receding goals which lure us on?

Take for example the goal of knowledge. At commencement time thousands of young people are graduated from college. We say they are educated. Are they really? Their graduation means only that they have met certain more or less arbitrary requirements set up by the college. But to say that they are educated in the sense that there is nothing else for them to learn, that they have exhausted the field of knowledge or explored its possibilities, would be absurd. Actually they have only begun. Nobody has ever been educated in the sense that he knew all there was to be known. What is more, nobody ever will be! Knowledge presents a receding goal. We never reach it. The man who comes nearest to being educated is he who is always learning, who counts not himself to have attained but presses on toward the goal which he knows he will never fully reach.

When Auguste Sabatier died, there were discovered in his desk plans for research which would have required two hundred years for their accomplishment. Had he been able to carry out these plans would he then have reached the end? I venture that, had he lived to be as old as Methuselah, he would still have confronted receding goals. Education is and always will be a relative term. Yet the strange fact is that while educationwise we should be terribly disturbed were we told, "Thus far and no further," religionwise we are disturbed because Christ sets no limits to our spiritual pioneering. But here, too, are goals we never fully reach.

Or have you considered the receding goals of science? Every year finds us pushing back the frontiers. We are talking now about traveling in interstellar space, making trips to the moon, for example. I would not put it beyond us. Let me make a prediction. It is a safe prediction, since neither you nor I will know whether it came true. However, "I predict" that, never mind how many millions of years man may remain on this planet, he will never lose his scientific curiosity. He will never get to the end of his quest, never reach the place where he has solved all the mysteries. He will still be pressing on. In the unattainable lies the secret of growth, the growth of our minds, the growth of our amazing technical development.

And of our spiritual growth, Luther said that a man never is a Christian, but is always becoming one. If Christianity were the kind of religion that accommodated itself to our ability or lack of it, if it were made to fit us like a suit of clothes, it would, no doubt, be a more comfortable religion. It would enhance our appearance. It would make us feel that, religiously speaking, we were up-to-date, quite presentable. But like a suit of clothes it would have not the slightest effect on our life, the growth or development of our character. It would leave us as it found us—finely enfolded in our weaknesses, our limitations, our sins.

That sort of religion would be quite inadequate. It would lack the first essential of all genuine religion, which is the redemption of our life. And that is effected not by having a religion that is like us, made to order so to speak, but unlike us. We need a religion that makes us aware of the difference between us and the God who transcends us, whose ways are not our ways, whose thoughts are not our thoughts. Religion must make us aware of what we are, and yet of what we may become as we "press toward the mark."

"Brethren, I count not myself to have apprehended." I believe the Master would say to him: "Don't be discouraged about that, Paul. You once had something you could reach. You kept the law faithfully when you were a Pharisee. And you became fed up with it. Here is a goal you will never fully reach. But in striving towards it your life will be transformed, enriched, and made fruitful."

Here then are two things to be said for our unattainable goal. It is inevitable, since Christ came to reveal to us the nature of the Holy God, who is "righteous in all His works," perfect in his being. It is indispensable, since only that which transcends us, transforms us.

There is a third observation. These unattainable goals are purposeful. They serve Christianity's primary purpose. Christianity has many byways, but one main road; many tributaries, but one main current. Its primary purpose is to confront us with God and to make us feel our need of him, our dependence on him. Only an unattainable goal can do that. "Who is sufficient for these things?" Paul asks. And he answers: "Our sufficiency is from God." (II Cor. 2:16; 3:5.)

Now just suppose the kind of religion we professed was within our own power to attain. Then if we were asked, "Who is sufficient for these things?" we would answer, "We are." That would put our self, our ego, rather than God, at the center of our life. It would engender pride rather than humility, self-righteousness rather than penitence. That kind of religion does not redeem us from our sins. It confirms us in them. Jesus found just that kind of religion when he came. Some of the Pharisees had it. Not all of them, to be sure. Some of them. One of them boastfully prayed: "God, I thank thee that I am not like other men, . . . I fast twice a week, I give tithes of all that I get." (Luke 18:11, 12.) "I fast twice a week." Many of us no doubt would not find that too easy. But it can be done with will power. Will power has been facetiously defined as "mind over platter." Or again, "I give tithes of all that I get." That too can be done. Some of us do it. It is not particularly difficult. Moreover, we find that we are in no sense impoverished when we give back to God at least a tenth of what he has given us.

These and similar demands of the law were kept by the Pharisees of old. Such was their religion. It is perhaps not unfair to say that the religion of the Pharisees was based on what man can do, not on what God helps man to do.

Christianity is not that kind of religion. It has a different purpose; namely, to make men feel their need of God, their dependence on him. We cannot be Christians just by our will power and determination, by rolling up our sleeves and blowing on our hands. Paul found that out. "To will is present with me; but how to perform that which is good I find not. For the good that I would I do not: but the evil which I would not, that I do." (Rom. 7:18-19 K.J.V.) When a man confronts that situation, then he turns to the God whom Christ revealed, the God of boundless grace and everlasting mercy. As Paul again writes, "For God has done what the law, weakened by the flesh, could not do." (Rom. 8:3)

How often have people said when asked to fill some office in the church, "Oh, I am not good enough!" That always seems to me the finest sort of qualification. Of course, you are not good enough! Speaking personally, if I were told that the requirement for my being in this pulpit was that I be good enough, I tell you honestly I would never stand here again. Of course, I am not good enough. But Christianity is not a religion that advertises human goodness. Christianity is a religion that proclaims God's boundless grace, unwearying love, and everlasting mercy and forgiveness. Christianity is not a religion based on what man can do, but on what God through Christ has done for man. "By grace you have been saved through faith; and this is not your own doing, it is the gift of God—not because of works, lest any man should boast." (Eph. 2:8, 9.) "The God who asks everything is eager also to give everything. His moral demands are absolute, but he forgives to the uttermost." "He is a God of grace as well as of truth." [2]

"Brethren, I count not myself to have apprehended: . . . I press toward the mark." And I believe the Master would say to his faithful apostle, "Do not be discouraged. Remember what you said once, 'Work out your own salvation . . . for God is at work in you.' (Phil. 2:12.) Remember, Paul, that you said, 'I can do all things in him who strengthens me.' (Phil. 4:13.) It is not where you are, Paul, at any given stage of the journey that is the test, but the direction in which you are moving, the goal for which you are striving. You are on the way to salvation as long as you can say, 'I press toward the mark.' "

[2] *Ibid.*, pp. 43, 44.

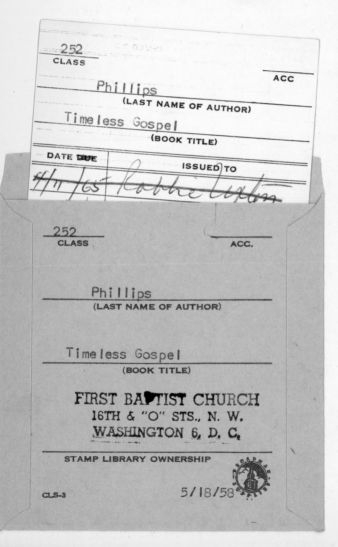

252
CLASS

ACC

Phillips
(LAST NAME OF AUTHOR)

Timeless Gospel
(BOOK TITLE)

DATE ~~DUE~~	ISSUED TO
4/11/65	*Rothe Luston*

252
CLASS

ACC.

Phillips
(LAST NAME OF AUTHOR)

Timeless Gospel
(BOOK TITLE)

FIRST BAPTIST CHURCH
16TH & "O" STS., N. W.
WASHINGTON 6, D. C.

CLS-3

5/18/58